DEC   2017

a SAVOR THE SOUTH® *cookbook*

Barbecue

a SAVOR THE SOUTH® *cookbook*

Barbecue

JOHN SHELTON REED

The University of North Carolina Press CHAPEL HILL

The paper in this book meets the guidelines for permanence and durability of
the Committee on Production Guidelines for Book Longevity of the Council on
Library Resources. The University of North Carolina Press has been a member
of the Green Press Initiative since 2003.

Jacket illustration: courtesy depositphotos.com/© yuratosno.

Library of Congress Cataloging-in-Publication Data
Reed, John Shelton, author.
Barbecue / John Shelton Reed.
pages cm — (A savor the South cookbook)
Includes index.
ISBN 978-1-4696-2670-3 (cloth : alk. paper)
ISBN 978-1-4696-2671-0 (ebook)
1. Barbecuing—Southern States. 2. Cooking, American—Southern style.
I. Title. II. Series: Savor the South cookbook.
TX840.B3R4445 2016   641.7′6—dc23
2015028000

Contents

a SAVOR THE SOUTH® *cookbook*

Barbecue

Introduction

o avoid any misunderstanding, let's get something straight up front. I'm not going to tell Koreans or Californians that their "barbecue" isn't. If someone in Seattle wants to "barbecue" salmon on a cedar plank, that's fine and I hope I'm invited. I won't even call out some Midwesterner in a "Kiss the Chef" apron who thinks he's barbecuing when he grills weenies in his backyard. Chacun a son 'cue, as the French might say, if they knew anything about the subject. But when food writer Jeffrey Steingarten said that barbecue is "simply the most delectable of all traditional American foods," he wasn't talking about that stuff. He meant *Southern* barbecue (or "barbeque," as it's often spelled in the South), and when I say "barbecue" so do I. That means meat cooked for a long time at a low temperature with heat and smoke from burning wood or wood coals. We'll come back to the question of what kind of meat, but "low and slow" cooking in the presence of wood smoke is pretty much what it's all about.

Of course, Southerners allow exceptions to every rule, and in this book you will encounter a few legendary barbecue places that cook hot and fast. But they don't compromise on that wood smoke. No one should compromise on that. Don't confuse the (ahem) sacred and propane. It's true that some scoundrels put barbecue sauce on oven-cooked meat and call it barbecue, but that's like putting kosher salt on it and calling it kosher. Barbecue isn't about sauce; in fact, for most Southerners sauce is almost an afterthought (which doesn't mean we're not ready to fight about it) and Texans often use no sauce at all. Sauce *is* a big deal in Missouri—one reason to question that state's Southern bona fides—but the Show Me State is in this book if only because it had a star in the Confederate flag. Yes, that was more the Confederacy's decision than Missouri's, but if it was good enough for Jefferson Davis it's good enough for me.

But I've digressed. That often happens when Southerners talk about barbecue—or anything else, for that matter. Back to the introduction.

Steingarten calls barbecue "the gaudiest jewel in the crown of the American South, where most of the finest traditional American cooking originated," and that's what this book is about: Southern barbecue and its usual accessories.

You don't have to tell me that the world doesn't need another barbecue cookbook. I own a couple of dozen. But this *series* needs a barbecue cookbook. So I've tried to make this as much educational as culinary, with recipes for traditional dishes or approximations of traditional dishes, often ones that illustrate some point about the development of regional styles of barbecue. These may not be the "best" recipes—they're not necessarily the tastiest and God forbid that they should be innovative—but they are *typical* ones. Plenty of those other cookbooks offer variations, and some of them are undoubtedly improvements. You might want to try them sometime, but first you should understand what they are variations on.

So, how did this gaudy jewel come to be? Or rather, since Southern barbecue is intensely local, how did these several gaudy jewels, this glorious mosaic, come to be? A little history is in order.

People have always and almost everywhere known that low and slow cooking is a good way to handle tough or gnarly meat, but we first encounter something Southerners would recognize as barbecue in the West Indies in the 1500s, where native Indians and Spanish newcomers had begun cooking European hogs on a sort of wooden frame that the Indians had formerly used for a miscellany of rodents, reptiles, and fish. In the 1690s a Dominican missionary observed that the Indians served the meat with a splash of lime juice and hot peppers. The Indians called the frame something that the Spanish heard as "barbacoa," from which the English took the word "barbecue" (so Yankees and Australians have a venerable precedent when they speak of putting something "on the barbecue"). Very quickly the word—though not immediately the sauce—migrated to the English colonies on the eastern seaboard of North America, where "barbecuing" came to mean cooking meat more or less Caribbean-style and big community "barbecues" continued a British hog-roast tradition. These occasions saw hogs, sheep, sides of beef, and many types of game—squirrels, possums, in Maryland even turtles—cooked over barbecue pits (literally pits, or trenches) full of live coals, then chopped or pulled apart by hand.

In the early colonial era these events were common as far north as New England, but by the time of the Revolution the community barbecue had become identified with the states from the Chesapeake region south to Georgia, where regular "barbecue days" brought out all sorts and conditions of citizenry to eat, drink, dance, and gamble. (George Washington won eight shillings playing cards at an Alexandria barbecue in 1769.) A young Virginian writing to a London friend in 1784 described a typical eighteenth-century barbecue: "It's a shoat & sometimes a Lamb or Mutton & indeed sometimes a Beef splitt into & stuck on spitts, & then they have a large Hole dugg in the ground where they have a number of Coals made of the Bark [?] of Trees, put in this Hole. & then they lay the Meat over that within about six inches of the Coals, & then they Keep basting it with Butter & Salt & Water & turning it every now and then, until it is done, we then dine under a large shady tree or an harbour made of green bushes, under which we have benches & seats to sit on when we dine sumptuously." This sounds great if you get to sit under the "harbour"— less so, of course, if you're a slave on the digging and basting crew.

Barbecues were also held to mark occasions like homecomings, reunions, and political campaigns, and to celebrate all manner of things. When news of the Treaty of Paris reached New Bern, North Carolina, for instance, a visiting Spanish army officer reported, "There was a barbecue (a roast pig) and a barrel of rum, from which the leading officials and citizens of the region promiscuously ate and drank with the meanest and lowest kind of people, holding hands and drinking from the same cup. It is impossible to imagine, without seeing it, a more purely democratic gathering." (Such democratic occasions were less popular in hierarchical South Carolina, where barbecue was often cooked and served in private clubs. This tradition has persisted: the bylaws of the Ellerton Farmers Club, which still meets regularly, specify that dinner at meetings "shall consist of cue, rice, hash, two kinds of bread, one salad, one pickle, coffee, and nothing more.")

The one thing missing from colonial-era barbecue was supplied early in the nineteenth century when someone brought that Caribbean lime juice and pepper seasoning to the mainland. Most likely it was slaves from the islands: the African influence on Southern cuisine (on Southern life, for that matter) has often been to make things spicier. A lemon juice version caught on quickly, and spread. Soon the lemon juice was supplemented or replaced by vinegar, more easily obtained in the temperate zone, and the result was a simple vinegar, pepper, and salt combination, perhaps with a secret pinch of this and a dash of that, used to mop the cooking meat and sprinkled on the resulting barbecue to season it.

Up until the twentieth century, Americans everywhere cooked a variety of domestic animals and game over pits, and mopped and served the meat with some version of that spicy vinegar-based sauce. Some kinds of meat were easier to come by in some places, and thus cooked more often, but there was no dogmatism about what constituted proper *barbecue*, the dish. In fact, the word wasn't commonly used that way until well into the nineteenth century. Any kind of meat could be barbecued anywhere, and a more or less uniform American Way of Barbecue could be found from the Atlantic coast to Texas and beyond.

But this consensus didn't last. The appropriate meat or meats and even what cuts to cook became matters first of geographic variation, then of local tradition. Since the middle of the twentieth century what's regarded in one place as the only real kind of barbecue might not even be recognized as barbecue in another. If you want ribs in the Carolinas, for instance, you go to a rib place—ribs aren't *barbecue*—and when Carolinians barbecue chicken (page 27), the result is barbecued chicken, not chicken barbecue. Just so, brisket is barbecue in Texas, for sure, but not in Kentucky, where mutton is.

Side dishes also became largely dictated by local tradition. Coleslaw, for instance, is almost universally available and in some parts virtually required. But whether it's made primarily with vinegar or mayonnaise and whether it includes any mustard or ketchup largely depends on where you are (see pages 81–86). Just so, some kind of bread made from cornmeal often comes with one's barbecue, but different kinds in different places (see pages 87–91), and elsewhere the bread of choice is sliced white bread straight from the wrapper. The story is similar for side-dish stews (pages 73–79), beans (pages 94–97), and potatoes (pages 100–102).

There's also no agreement when it comes to what sauce to use, if any. More often than not, usually by a process of evolution, the once-ubiquitous vinegar-and-pepper sauce—the Mother Sauce (page 59)—has been replaced by something else. A fateful development occurred when the Centennial Exposition of 1876 in Philadelphia introduced America to bottled tomato ketchup. By coincidence that same exposition brought us kudzu from Japan; soon both the vine and the condiment were found everywhere in the South, and it was only a matter of time before someone tinkered with barbecue sauce.

Various combinations of meat and sauce now define several major barbecue regions and a great many microregions. The church of barbecue has splintered into many denominations— South Carolina alone now boasts four distinct sauce regions— and, as in the original Reformation, Germans played a prominent role.

In eastern North Carolina and the adjoining part of South Carolina, the word "barbecue" now means only pork, but otherwise these areas have been bypassed by the evolution I mentioned and barbecue is still pretty much what it has been for the last 200 years: whole hogs cooked and served with the classic vinegar-and-pepper sauce.

As you head west across North Carolina these days, however, somewhere around the middle of the state the sauce gets redder and sweeter. That's because around the time of the First World War a number of barbecue stand operators in the Lexington and Salisbury area began adding ketchup to the classic vinegar-and-pepper sauce as a flavoring and coloring agent. I believe it's no accident that nearly all of them had German names. They also starting cooking pork shoulders instead of whole hogs, and, with their compatriot Mr. Heinz's ketchup, what they wound up with was a barbecue version of a traditional German dish.

The story is similar in South Carolina. Areas in the Piedmont where barbecue is now pork shoulder and the sauce includes a tincture of ketchup are areas where Germans settled. Moreover, a swath of the state from Columbia in the middle to Charleston on the coast boasts a unique yellow, mustard-based sauce (page 62), and the names attached to restaurants that serve it and bottlers who sell it make it obvious that it's those Germans again.

Germans also figure in the Kentucky barbecue story, particularly in the area around Owensboro, where Catholic parish barbecues have preserved a mutton tradition that has disappeared almost everywhere else. Many of those Catholics are of German descent, and it's significant that many older patrons of the local barbecue restaurants prefer their mutton (page 31) served with rye bread.

But nowhere is the German influence more obvious than in central Texas, where nineteenth-century German and Czech settlers started meat markets like those back home, selling fresh pork and beef and sausage, and smoking their leftovers in brick smokers with separate fireboxes, as they had done in Europe. Food writer Robb Walsh remarks that they must have been bemused when black migrant cotton pickers took their smoked meat for barbecue and started eating it on butcher paper with crackers and pickles. When Texas's old-fashioned pit-cooked barbecue places came under pressure from twentieth-century health regulations, many of them switched to German-style smokers. "And so," Walsh writes, "the old meat markets came to be considered the quintessential Texas barbecue joints—despite the fact that the German smoked meats and sausages they originally produced weren't really barbecue at all."

Those black migrant workers brought their taste for smoked meat west from the Deep South, where yet another barbecue tradition had become established. I wish I could find some Germans in that tradition's ancestral woodpile, but I can't. What's obvious in the barbecue of the old cotton belt is the African American contribution. Black slaves did most of the barbecuing on the old plantation, cooking whole hogs both for the Big House and (often surreptitiously) for themselves, and barbecue has been the stuff of song and story in the Deep South ever since those days. For whatever reason—perhaps because white folks were less likely to want the tough or bony parts, even when transformed by low and slow cooking—shoulders and ribs became popular cuts in the black community, first as products of whole-hog cooking, but eventually as the stand-alone raw material for barbecue stands and restaurants. Until the 1900s, Deep South barbecue was mopped and sauced with the Mother Sauce, and some outposts of tradition still do it that way. Elsewhere some cooks have devised their own idiosyncratic sauces (see, for example, page 64). But for most places in the Southern interior these days, what goes on ribs and pulled pork shoulder is no longer vinegar with stuff in it but ketchup with stuff in it—thick, red, and sweet (often *very* sweet—see page 63).

Memphis is the unofficial capital of the Mississippi Delta, what historian James Cobb calls "the most Southern place on earth," so it's not surprising that its barbecue exemplifies the Deep South style, with a ketchup-based sauce (page 65) and an emphasis on pork shoulder and ribs. With nearly 200 barbecue places listed in its Yellow Pages, Memphis is a major barbecue center, home to the annual Memphis-in-May World Championship Barbecue Cooking Contest. But it is also a big city, with the ethnic diversity that implies, and when the pork barbecue of the Deep South came to town it ran up against Italian and Greek restaurateurs who added their own twists. The result was only-in-Memphis dishes like "barbecue pizza," pulled pork shoulder in spaghetti sauce (page 40), and spare ribs rubbed with oregano and thyme (page 54).

Finally, one other significant Southern barbecue tradition is a recent one. Kansas City's barbecue scene dates from a rib stand opened in 1908 by a newcomer from the Memphis area, and the Kansas City barbecue of today has clearly evolved from the Memphis style, with a few Texas licks thrown in. Over 100 restaurants in the city now serve it. Kansas City's "polyamorous" barbecue, as food writer Hanna Raskin calls it, mixes and matches all sorts of meats with a variety of sauces, the most popular being like a Deep South sauce—thick, ketchupy, and sweet (page 68).

Ardie A. Davis, a Kansas Citian, claims that his city's style is and will remain "at the epicenter of American barbecue," and he may be right. Kansas City came late to the barbecue party, but it has lately taken over the invitations. Every year the Kansas City Barbeque Society hosts the American Royal Invitational, a cook-off they immodestly call the "World Series of Barbecue." The KCBS is also the principal sponsor of barbecue competitions nationally, so naturally Kansas City–style barbecue always wins. (If you use a vinegar or mustard sauce, lots of luck. If you don't use a sauce at all, God help you.) Kansas City's pick-your-meat, pick-your-sauce, International House of Barbecue style is also what you find in chain restaurants and in new independent restaurants wherever there is no local tradition to inoculate against it, and it's even beginning to overwhelm the defenses of those places that do have their own styles.

This may be the future, but for now America's barbecue landscape is delightfully diverse; local traditions still reflect varying physical environments, farming practices, and historical settlement patterns. Years ago I wrote, "Barbecue is the nearest thing we have in the United States to Europe's wines and cheeses: Drive a hundred miles and the barbecue changes." But soon, perhaps, if you drive a hundred miles, or a thousand, the barbecue *won't* change. It will be as uniform as it was in the nineteenth century. Ketchup will have triumphed everywhere.

Another possibility, however, is not uniformity but dizzying variety. Maybe the barbecue will change if you just go around the corner, or come back next week.

Until recently, barbecue hasn't been about innovation. Barbecue men (and they've nearly all been men) have been like Orthodox icon painters. Some were more accomplished than others, but what they produced was established by tradition. Self-expression has been thought uncalled for; culinary creativity has been unnecessary, if not actually undesirable. Lately, however, barbecue has begun to appear on the menus of surprisingly high-toned restaurants, restaurants with wine lists and valet parking, where it's being cooked by actual chefs who just can't resist adding cheffy touches. Blueberry in sauces, ground coffee in rubs—that sort of thing. There's nothing intrinsically wrong with this, and much of it tastes pretty good, but this trend is yet another reason to be concerned about the future of local barbecue traditions.

For barbecue's first few hundred years, it was only rarely "home cooking." Before the appearance of stands that sold it retail, barbecue was pretty much limited to community and institutional events, because the process typically produced large quantities of cooked meat that required large numbers of eaters. Even after refrigeration made that less of a problem, most people were content to leave barbecue to the professionals because (as you may discover) it's not easy to cook. If barbecuing at home is experiencing a vogue these days, it's largely because it is a challenge. Chris Schlesinger, a Virginian who cooked barbecue at his East Coast Grill in Cambridge, Massachusetts, says, "I think making your own barbecue is on the outer edge of what can be done in home cooking. You can do it, but it's a real effort."

In the nineteenth century most Southern communities could boast a master barbecue cook or two, often black men, who supervised the labor, monitored the temperature, determined when to add more coals and where to place them, decided when to mop the meat, and finally declared the process complete. These men learned their craft by years of apprenticeship. These days, many of us would have a hard time finding a master who would take us on, and most of us don't have time for that, anyway. But to preserve local barbecue traditions it may be necessary to translate them for home production. Hence, this book.

Let me say a word about what's not in it.

To "savor the South," you should taste what Southerners cook and other people don't (or what they copy from Southerners). So you'll find no recipes here for salmon, duck, or tofu. Maybe I'll put them in the twentieth edition if we somehow make these dishes our own, but not yet. It was more tempting to include examples of certain ethnic barbecue-like dishes that are increasingly part of the Southern scene: Vietnamese *banh mi*, Cantonese *char siu*, Korean *kalbi* and *bulgogi*, Mexican *carne asada* or *barbacoa* (the original Spanish word, now attached to something rather like a luau). But these, too, still have a way to go before they belong in a book about Southern barbecue.

There's also nothing here about things Southerners no longer cook. Newspapers used to report barbecues with hundreds of squirrels in the starring role, for instance, and barbecued possum was once the stuff of stereotype, but there's not much call for those recipes these days, so I haven't provided any.

I've been inconsistent when it comes to types of barbecue and side dishes that are found only in Southern microregions. Kentucky mutton is here (pages 31 and 71), and so are snoots from the St. Louis area (page 38), Memphis "dry ribs" (page 54), Cajun cochon de lait (page 42), and Gulf Coast smoked mullet (page 45). I've included South Carolina's yellow sauce (page 62) and North Alabama's white (page 70), as well as some extremely localized side dishes like boiled potatoes from eastern North Carolina and hot tamales from the Mississippi Delta and vicinity (page 98). They're here for their historical importance or just their weirdness. But the smoked precooked "city ham" found in western Kentucky; eastern Missouri's grilled "pork steak" (sliced from a shoulder and basted or even braised with a thick, sweet red sauce); or the ham cooked fast, sliced very thin (basically "chipped"), and served on a bun with a Kansas City–style sauce in upper East Tennessee—these dishes get only this mention.

Finally, one omission deserves special explanation. I have not included instructions for cooking a whole hog. This may seem very strange indeed since, as food writer Jim Auchmutey observes, whole hog is "where the Southern train left the station" and where the mystique of the pitmaster was born. But there's not room in this little book for a multipage protocol, and there's probably not room in your cooker for a hog: An entire porker requires a hog-sized cooker or at least a big hole in the ground. Also, if you mess it up you've wasted a lot of time and money. Frankly, I leave whole-hog cooking to the professionals, and you might want to do the same. If you do want to play in the big leagues, good luck, but I'd urge you to start with a few shoulders. When you're pretty sure you're ready to cook a hog, videos aplenty on the web will show you how, sort of, or (since you're reading this and seem to be a holdover from the Age of Literacy) you can find instructions in a number of Southern cookbooks. William McKinney provides some, for instance, in *Holy Smoke: The Big Book of North Carolina Barbecue*. My wife and I had a hand in that book, but I confess that my favorite instructions are from someone else's: In *Entertainments*, the gourmet and food writer Judith Olney begins, "First shoot the pig." Anyway, although videos and books are no substitute for an apprenticeship with a grizzled East Carolina pitmaster, they'll get you started.

The recipes in this book for preparing sauces, breads, side dishes, and so forth are pretty straightforward, but cooking barbecue is another matter. You'll probably need a few words on barbecuing technique. More than a few, actually.

Many forms of barbecue have traditionally been prepared with direct heat—that is, cooked above burning coals, usually at some distance—but more common these days for home cooking (and almost universal in barbecue competitions) is *indirect* heat, with the fire off to the side or even in a separate chamber altogether. To be sure, the distinction is not always that clear in practice: Pete Jones, a celebrated eastern North Carolina traditionalist, once said, "We put our coals around the pig, never under it—that is, if you want to do it right." Nevertheless, direct heat is the old-fashioned way. That's the point of the pit in pit barbecue. That's how the Caribbean Indians did it.

You could do it, too. For that matter, if you're into historic re-enactment you could burn down hardwood in a separate fireplace and shovel the glowing coals under the meat. Real Americans used to do that, and some of the greatest barbecue restaurants still do. With only a couple of exceptions, though, the recipes in this book call for indirect heat, produced by commercial lump charcoal or briquettes out of a bag, with a few soaked wood chunks (oak or hickory) added to produce more smoke. In my opinion, that is an acceptable compromise for the home cook (but let's not forget that it is a compromise).

Cooking with a gas grill and a pan full of wood chips is even more of a compromise—too much of one, if you ask me. If you're going to be lazy about it, why not just cook up some faux 'cue in your oven or crockpot, and maybe add some liquid smoke to the sauce. You won't have to worry about the temperature and you'll get to stay indoors. I'm not going to tell you how to cheat, though. You'll have to figure that out for yourself.

Here's what you'll need to cook the barbecue in this book:

1. *A cooker*, obviously. Ideally it should have a cover, although in a pinch you can make your own with heavy-duty aluminum foil. Fancy cookers with offset fireboxes are great if they're not too flimsy (many are), but cookers that stack a grill over a pan of liquid over a pan of coals within a domed cylinder work just fine. So do "kettle" cookers, if they're large enough to put the meat on one side and the coals and wood chunks on the other. (You might as well add an aluminum-foil cake pan full of water or cider or beer under the meat, to keep things moist.)

2. *Two thermometers.* You need one for the temperature in the cooker (do not trust any built-in thermometer, no matter how much you paid for the cooker) and one to measure the internal temperature of the meat. Ideal are thermometers with sensors you can leave inside the cooker and gauges you can read outside. That way you don't have to keep opening the cooker to see what's going on. High-tech rednecks have remote-read thermometers that let you go about your business (or stay in bed) while the barbecue cooks, but some of us think that sitting by the cooker for

a few hours, maybe drinking a beer or six, is part of the process.

3. *A starter chimney for the charcoal.* Trust me. You'll wonder why you ever fooled with lighter fluid. Put charcoal in the top half, wad up a couple of sheets of newspaper in the bottom, light the paper, and watch the magic.

4. *Gloves.* Get stout suede-palmed work gloves or the expensive insulated kind. Trying to handle big chunks of meat with tongs or a fork is just stupid.

5. *A small mop or squirt bottle* for basting, if you're going to baste.

6. *Heavy-duty aluminum foil.* Lots of it. Even if you don't use "the Texas crutch" (page 19), you might want to wrap the meat at the end to keep it warm, and lining your cooker with foil makes cleanup easier.

7. *A wire brush/scraper tool,* or something like it (speaking of cleanup).

Barbecuing is not like oven-cooking. You can't say things like "Put it in a 225° oven for two and a half hours." The temperature in your cooker is probably going to go up and down. It may be different at the thermometer and at the surface of the meat. How long it will take to barbecue a piece of meat depends on its size and starting temperature, what kind of cooker you have, the outside temperature, and even the wind speed (seriously). Most of these recipes give a cooking temperature or a range of temperatures to aim for, but don't worry too much if you miss the mark. There's lots of room for error. If the temperature is too low, cooking takes longer, that's all. If it's too high, you're almost certainly not going to burn the meat, and you can probably find authorities who would tell you to cook at that temperature anyway. To lower the temperature, open the cooker for a while. To raise it, open the vent (if you have one) to supply more air to the fire, or add a few more (lit) coals.

Given all this indeterminacy, when these recipes give cooking times they're only approximate. Don't blame me if an estimate is off, even way off. The meat isn't done until it's done. Old-timers can tell when that is by touch and feel, but you're not an old-timer, are you? *Use your meat thermometer* and cook until the internal temperature reaches the level the recipe calls for. Thermometers usually don't work for pork ribs, but even there you go by "feel," not time.

Seriously, do give yourself plenty of time. Nothing is sadder than undercooked barbecue. If you finish early, the meat can sit happily wrapped in foil in a cooler or a turned-off oven until time to serve, and it may even be the better for it. (By the way, don't be alarmed if your cooked meat is pink near the surface. That's the "smoke ring," created by wood-cooking, and it's a *good* thing.)

Finally, never forget that this is supposed to be fun. If you're not enjoying yourself, pack it in. Cooking barbecue is too much trouble not to have a good time while you're at it. Of course, if you stick it out, you'll have some seriously good eating. Not only that, you'll be helping to preserve some splendid traditions. If you're a Southerner this will put you in touch with your heritage. If you're not, here's your chance to pretend you are.

Meats

Let's skip the appetizers and get straight to the main course. Forget the hokey pokey: this is what it's all about. Without meat, time, and wood smoke, all you have are the ingredients for a Methodist covered-dish supper.

Pan-Southern Pork Shoulder

Pork shoulder is the most forgiving of barbecue meats. It's self-basting, it develops a wonderfully smoky "bark," and it's hard to overcook. It's a good place for beginners to start and not a bad place to stop, which is probably why it's found chopped, pulled, or sliced on barbecue plates and sandwiches almost everywhere in the South. Even in mutton and beef country it's usually offered as an alternative. What differs from place to place are the rubs, mops, and sauces. (We'll get to those.)

A pork shoulder has two parts. The bottom is the "picnic ham" and the top is the "Boston butt" (yet it has no connection to the hog's hams or butt, being found at the opposite end). Few grocery stores carry intact shoulders, but you can almost always buy the two components and put them back together, or you can just cook a Boston butt or two. A butt is obviously smaller than a whole shoulder, and many say it is the better half.

Here's how to cook a shoulder or butt. After you've read the rest of this book, you can rub, mop, and sauce it in whatever regional style you choose.

SERVES — *well, a shoulder or Boston butt cooked and deboned will usually yield 50–60 percent of its original weight, so a 12-pound shoulder, for instance, will give you 6 or 7 pounds of barbecue. How many that will serve depends on how hungry they are.*

---

1 pork shoulder (or Boston butt)
Rub of your choice
Mop of your choice (optional)
Sauce of your choice (optional)

Apply the rub generously and let the meat sit for at least an hour (ideally overnight), refrigerated. Put the meat in your cooker "face"-side (not "skin"-side) down and cook at 210–250°. Mop it hourly, if desired, but do not turn the meat. When the internal temperature reaches at least 180° for slicing, or 190° for "pulling" or chopping (at least 6 hours, maybe as much as 10), remove the meat from the cooker, wrap it loosely in foil, and let it rest for at least a half hour.

Pull it with forks or your fingers, chop it with a cleaver on a block, or slice it, removing bone, fat, and gristle. If you're chopping or pulling, mix the "outside brown" throughout. If sauce is used, it can be added sparingly while you're chopping or pulling, it can be set out at the table for eaters to add themselves, or both. Serve it on a plate, in a sandwich, or some other way (see page 40, for instance).

Righteous Ribs

Although there are exceptions (see, for example, page 54), most Southerners cook their pork ribs "low and slow" and put sauce on them. Cooked that way, any advantages of baby back ribs disappear, so get some proper spareribs (not "country ribs"—which aren't actually ribs). Spareribs are cheaper and more flavorful, and, besides, baby back ribs sound like they're for sissies. A rack of ribs can be manicured "St. Louis style" to make it prettier and the ribs more uniform. If you want to throw good meat away for cosmetic purposes, you can buy it this way or do it yourself (Google "St. Louis style trim").

This is one of the few cases where you can't use a meat thermometer to decide when you're done, because the meat is too thin. So pick up the rack with tongs or gloves and see if it flops. When the meat cracks a bit, you can stop—or not. Competition barbecuers say ribs that "fall off the bone" are overdone, but don't let them boss you around: Some people prefer them that way.

You can choose your rubs and sauces to cook ribs Alabama, Memphis, or Kansas City style.

3- to 5-pound rack of spareribs for every 1–2 eaters
Cooking oil
Rub of your choice (2–3 tablespoons per rack)
Sauce of your choice

Rinse the ribs and pat them dry with a paper towel. Remove the membrane from the back: just stick a screwdriver or butter knife under it and wiggle it off. Coat each rack with cooking oil, sprinkle the rub over both sides, and rub it in. Let it sit, refrigerated, for at least 2 hours (overnight is fine).

Barbecue, meat-side up, with indirect heat and wood smoke (see pages 11–13) at approximately 225° for about 5 hours. Check for doneness (see above). When done, paint with the sauce while still hot. Serve with additional sauce on the side.

Texas Monthly Brisket

Smoked brisket may be one of the many German contributions to Texas barbecue. Although its status as a Lone Star icon apparently dates only from the middle of the last century, it has now become for central Texas what whole hog is for eastern North Carolina: the real test of a cook's skill and almost the definition of "barbecue."

Brisket can be tricky because it comes in two parts: the "flat" and the "point," and it's easy to overcook the flat or undercook the point. The flat is the larger piece that, confusingly, comes to a point; it's leaner, and it's, well, sort of flat. The point is a fattier lump that sits atop the unpointy end of the flat, separated from it by a vein of fat. The point isn't as pretty and it doesn't slice as well, but some of us think that's where the taste of brisket is concentrated.

Of course, opinions differ about the right way to cook this cut. Some marinate it as long as overnight; others don't marinate at all. Some mop the meat, some don't. Reputable cooks have been observed cooking at temperatures ranging from 200° to as high as 600°. Some serve the finished product with sauce ladled on top, most don't.

One big disagreement is that some wrap a brisket in aluminum foil after 4–6 hours to keep it from drying out, while others sneer that it won't get too dry if you cook it right. Kansas City pitmaster Paul Kirk calls foil "the Texas crutch," and for once I side with KC against Texas: Foil wrap does make your brisket moister, but it also tends to make it taste like pot roast.

Here's how Daniel Vaughn does it. He's the barbecue editor of Texas Monthly, *so this is as close to canonical as you're going to get. Notice that Vaughn uses more-permeable butcher paper instead of foil. (He says "foil is for braising, and this recipe is for smoking.")*

In Texas, brisket is usually cooked in a smoker with a separate firebox in which oak or hickory wood is burned, but you can cook with indirect heat from charcoal, using wood chunks for smoke. Don't mess with the meat: You don't need to turn, flip, poke, prod, or even look at it.

Vaughn uses a "Dalmatian" rub that's simply 4 parts freshly ground black pepper to 1 part kosher salt. (If you're using already-ground black pepper, get the coarse variety and use a lot more: one storied Texas barbecue place uses a 9 to 1 ratio.) Other Texans add just some paprika or cayenne for a little heat, as in the rub on page 51.

By the way, brisket is also cooked in Kansas City. If you want to replicate that style, substitute the appropriate rub (page 52) and add sauce (page 68).

SERVES 10–12

10–12 pound well-marbled brisket with the fat cap still intact
Rub of your choice (see above)

Trim the fat to ¼–½ inch thick, leaving a continuous layer on the top of the brisket. Dry the meat and apply the rub generously to all surfaces. Let the meat stand at room temperature until the rub draws out enough moisture from the meat to look wet (at least ½ hour).

Fill a pan with water and put it near the fire. Put the brisket in the smoker with the fat-side up and the thick end toward the fire. Cook at 225–250°, adding water to the pan if necessary. When the interior temperature reaches 185–190°, wrap the brisket tightly in unwaxed butcher paper, return it to the cooker, then raise the smoker temperature to 275–300° and cook until the underside of the brisket is tender to the touch. (The fat on top will get done before the meat at the bottom.) Allow at least an hour per pound (that is, 10–12 hours), but aiming to finish a few hours ahead of serving is wise, in case of glitches.

When the meat is done, remove it from the cooker and let it rest for at least half an hour. After its rest, you can put it in a cooler or unheated oven where it will stay warm for 3–4 hours with no problem.

When you're ready to serve, separate the flat and the point. Do not remove the delicious fat cap. Slice the flat with the fat-side up, against the grain, into roughly ⅜-inch slices. Slice the point similarly, or chop it for chopped brisket sandwiches, or put it aside for burnt ends (next recipe).

Burnt Ends, KC Style

Burnt ends are a Kansas City thing. Originally just the debris left after a brisket was carved, especially the crisp, smoky edges of the fatty "point" portion, they used to be given away at Arthur Bryant's Barbecue. Eventually other Kansas City restaurants began mixing these flavorsome leftovers with barbecue sauce and serving them as a dish in their own right, and demand soon exceeded supply. Ingenious restaurateurs found ways to provide their customers with burnt pseudo-ends, and if you want more burnt ends from your brisket than the Lord intended, here's the best of the ways they do it. Personally, I think using the point to make burnt ends amounts to deliberately overcooking the best-tasting (if not the best-looking) part of the brisket, but suit yourself.

Since you're starting with meat that has already been barbecued, you can do this one in your oven, if you want.

ALLOW ABOUT A THIRD OF A POUND FOR A SANDWICH,
MAYBE HALF A POUND FOR A PLATE

---

1 brisket point, fully cooked with Kansas City Rub (page 52)
Kaycee "Red Menace" Sauce (page 68)

Cut the meat into 1-inch cubes, brush them with sauce, and cook at 225–230° until falling-apart tender (2–4 hours). Remove the meat from the cooker, wrap it in foil, and let it rest for at least 30 minutes. Mix the meat with a little sauce, and serve the result either as a dish or in a sandwich. It also makes a good addition to beans or gumbo.

Stockman Shoulder Clod

Shoulder clod is the bovine equivalent of pork shoulder—tough muscle and fat—and it is even more in need of a good long cook. Parts if it are often braised for pot roast, but clod was also the go-to cut of beef for Texas barbecue cooks until it was displaced by brisket (page 19) not that long ago. Weighing in at 20–25 pounds, this is one Texas-size hunk of meat. Sometimes it's sold as "chuck roast," but the same term is applied to various bits of the whole.

Cowboy barbecue uses direct heat, and right much of it: The meat is typically placed 2–3 feet above the coals and mopped while cooking to slow things down. The meat markets of central Texas also cook clod, but with indirect heat. I suggest you do the same, keep things relatively cool, and skip the mop.

Consider cutting the meat in half, to speed things up a bit, and allow yourself at least an hour per pound.

YIELDS 15–19 POUNDS OF COOKED MEAT

---

1 (20- to 25-pound) shoulder clod
Texas Beef Rub (page 51)
Lone Star Sauce (optional—see page 66)

Apply the rub generously and let the meat sit at room temperature for at least 2 hours before cooking. (Overnight is better.) Barbecue at 220–250° to an internal temperature of 160°, then wrap the meat in butcher paper and continue cooking to 190°. Wrap the meat loosely in foil and let it rest for at least 2 hours. It can then be sliced and dunked in sauce, if desired. Leftovers can be pulled or chopped for tacos, chili, stews, omelets, what have you.

West Texas Beef Ribs

Some cutesy restaurants serve beef ribs as "dinosaur bones," and it's true that there's nothing dainty about them, but it's a mistake to think of them as a bigger, cheaper, tougher version of pork ribs. They are, in effect, bits of rib-eye steak with a handle, and they're a staple in Texas and Oklahoma cow country. In other places they're sometimes viewed as scrap and trimmed so close that good, meaty ribs can be hard to find, but perseverance will be rewarded. (Be sure to ask for "back ribs," however, not short ribs.)

Leave the membrane on the backside intact: there's no argument about this (unlike with pork ribs). Southwestern beef ribs are served with a thin dipping sauce after they've been cooked to well-done. If you want your beef medium-rare, grill a steak.

START WITH A HALF-SLAB PER PERSON

2 slabs of beef ribs (cut to half slabs, if desired)
Texas Beef Rub (page 51)
Lone Star Sauce (page 66)

Apply the rub generously to the ribs. Place them in a cooker meat-side down and barbecue at 250–300°, with hickory or oak wood for smoke, for 1 hour; then turn them meat-side up. If there's enough meat to insert your thermometer, cook to an internal temperature of 155–160°; otherwise, cook for another 1½–2 hours until the meat has retreated a half inch or more up the bone and comes away from it if you give the rack a little twist.

Let the ribs rest for 5–10 minutes and serve them with the Lone Star Sauce on the side for dipping.

Hill Country Hot Guts

Texas sausage is usually forthright. For stuff like oregano and fennel in your links you have to go to Kansas City or Chicago. Robb Walsh's Legends of Texas Barbecue *reports that the "Bohunk sausage" served by Vencil Mares at the Taylor Cafe calls for nothing but meat, salt, and black pepper. Green's in Houston adds a little garlic powder and paprika. Places with a German heritage may throw in some mustard seeds. Dose it with red pepper and you have what Texans call "hot guts." But that's about it.*

Hot guts are identified with Elgin (hard g), the legislature-designated Sausage Capital of Texas, and the big two in Elgin are Southside Market & Barbecue (since 1882) and Meyer's Elgin Sausage (only since 1949). They are big: Southside Market sells something like two million pounds of sausage a year. To appeal to the wimpy mass market they took a lot of the heat out of hot guts back in the 1970s, but most Texas places that serve the still-very-warm guts put hot sauce on the table so you can put it back in, and other, smaller butchers and meat markets scattered around the Hill Country still do it the old way. The cayenne in this recipe provides plenty of heat for the average palate, but if you want that old-time sear, increase the amount or add hot sauce at the table.

The classic hot gut is all beef, but Texas sausages can be all beef, all pork, or (like these) something in between. For that matter, they can be venison, goat, or even turkey. But whatever the meat, the secret to success is that you can't have too much fat. Add it if you need to. One recipe I've seen calls for 7 pounds of beef and 3 pounds of beef fat.

If you're a novice, you might think about buying a sausage-making kit online and adapting it, but if you want to do it yourself from scratch, here's how.

25 feet of medium-size (32–35 mm) hog casings
6 pounds pork (fatty, boned Boston butt)
4 pounds beef (chuck or round roast, with fat)
¼ cup kosher salt
¼ cup freshly ground black pepper
¼ cup crushed red pepper
2 tablespoons cayenne pepper
8 garlic cloves, minced (or 1 teaspoon garlic powder)

Rinse the casings thoroughly under cold water, inside and out. Soak them overnight in a weak vinegar solution (1 tablespoon per cup of water). Coarse-grind the meats and knead to mix in the other ingredients. Refrigerate the mixture overnight.

Stuff the casings and tie off with string every 4 inches to make links. Uncooked links can be kept for a few days in the refrigerator or for up to 6 months frozen.

When you're ready to cook, heat the cooker to 225°. Rub the sausages lightly with vegetable oil and cook them to an interior temperature of 160–165° (approximately 2 hours—they should look about ready to burst).

Barbecued Chicken Two Ways

While barbecuing is far and away the best way to cook brisket, pork shoulder, and even turkey, it's less obvious that the same is true for chicken. But the barbecued chicken at Big Bob Gibson's in Decatur, Alabama, and B's Barbecue in Greenville, North Carolina, can be mentioned without much of a stretch in the same sentence as Edna Lewis's fried or Jacques Pépin's roasted. B's chicken is quite different from Big Bob's, but both are worth going a long way for, and you can produce something more or less like them at home.

The birds will cook more evenly if you halve them, the way they do at Big Bob's. Hold the chicken breast-side down and remove the backbone by cutting along both sides of the backbone with kitchen shears, crunching through the ribs. Then use the shears to cut the bird in half.

For moister chicken and an extra layer of tangy flavor, consider putting the uncooked chicken halves in a plastic bag with salted buttermilk (2 tablespoons salt per quart of buttermilk); leave them in the refrigerator overnight, then pat dry with paper towels. Notice that Big Bob's cooks at a higher temperature, which makes for crispier skin.

2 (3½–4) pound chickens, cut in half

FOR B'S
2 quarts Mother Sauce (page 59)
1 tablespoon kosher salt
2 teaspoons freshly ground black pepper

Sprinkle both sides of each half generously with the salt and pepper. Barbecue, skin-side up, at 230–240° until the temperature in the thigh reaches 180° (4–5 hours). Mop the skin side every 30 minutes and the open side at 1½ and 3 hours. Do not turn the chicken.

FOR BIG BOB'S
Approximately 1 quart North Alabama White Sauce (page 70)
1 tablespoon kosher salt
Cooking oil
2 teaspoons freshly ground black pepper

Sprinkle both sides of each half generously with the salt. Barbecue, skin-side up, at 325° until the skin is browned (about 1½ hours). Mop both sides with oil and turn the skin-side down. Sprinkle the open side generously with the pepper. Continue cooking until the temperature in the thigh reaches 180° (about another 1½ hours). Remove the chicken from the heat and dunk it immediately in a pot of white sauce (or slather the bird with sauce).

Liquid Margarine Smoked Turkey

Whole barbecued turkeys don't turn up often in restaurants, competitions, or the historical record. This is not because turkeys don't taste better barbecued than oven-roasted or even deep-fried (they really do), but because lots of us think they're not worth the trouble. If you're into pointless challenges, though, give it a try. Even if you're not, there may be times like Thanksgiving when nothing else will do.

The problem is that turkey breast has no fat and tends to be dry. It will be dry for sure if you overcook it to get the thighs done, so the easy way out is to do what many barbecue restaurants do, and cook just breasts or just legs. But if you want a whole fowl, consider the high-tech solution, which is to shoot the bird—(sorry) to inject the turkey with some sort of fat or oil. I do it, and I'm an old-fashioned guy who usually thinks hypodermics are for baseball players.

You don't have to, though. You can apply the lubricant externally, as a marinade. (Remember those nineteenth-century mops that included lard or butter?) Wishbone Italian dressing is a popular ingredient, but my buddy Johnny Bell prefers to start with liquid margarine and add his own seasoning. If the idea of liquid margarine grosses you out, use vegetable oil.

Start with a fresh turkey or a frozen one with no salt added, thoroughly thawed in the refrigerator (unless you like to live dangerously). Give yourself plenty of time: a frozen 12-pound turkey can take two days to thaw.

The carcass makes great stock for soup or gumbo.

1 (12-pound turkey), untrussed and giblets removed
4 tablespoons butter, melted (optional)

FOR THE SLATHER
1 (24-ounce) bottle liquid margarine (or vegetable oil)
1 tablespoon lemon pepper
1 tablespoon seasoned salt (Lawry's is the classic,
    but almost any will do)
⅓ cup sausage seasoning (store-bought or from below)

FOR THE SAUSAGE SEASONING (MIX THOROUGHLY)
1 tablespoon kosher salt
1 tablespoon dried sage
1 tablespoon dried thyme
1 tablespoon packed light brown sugar
1½ teaspoons freshly ground black pepper
1 teaspoon nutmeg
1 teaspoon crushed red pepper
½ teaspoon dried rosemary

FOR THE DRIP PAN
Any combination of water, cider, beer, or cola drink

Mix the slather in a bowl and apply it generously to the turkey, inside and out. Refrigerate the slathered bird in a sealed plastic trash bag, 24–36 hours. (Optional: Inject melted butter at 1½-inch intervals, concentrating on the breast.)

Cook the turkey breast-side up at 325° over a filled drip pan until the internal temperature of the breast is 165° (3 hours or more). Let it rest for half an hour before carving.

Daviess County Mutton-Style Lamb

Mutton used to be cooked at community barbecues everywhere, but now it's rarely found outside a microregion centered on Daviess County, Kentucky. The county seat, Owensboro, claims to be "the Barbecue Capital of the World," which is absurd, of course, but if it just called itself the mutton barbecue capital no one would argue. The Moonlite Bar-B-Q Inn is only the biggest of several restaurants that serve mutton; every summer local Catholic churches cook it for up to 5,000 hungry citizens at parish barbecues; and more than ten tons are served at a "Mutton Glutton" party during Owensboro's International Bar-B-Q Festival.

These days, however, mutton is not to everyone's taste, so why not start with lamb? It'll give you the idea, but it's less . . . assertive. It's also easier to acquire in most places. And although you could replicate the community barbecue experience by cooking a whole beast, most Kentuckians these days cook shoulders and maybe you should, too. (Incidentally, leg of lamb may be better for roasting and serving medium rare, but the fattier shoulder is better for fall-off-the-bone tenderness. It's cheaper, too.)

1 bone-in lamb shoulder (about 8 pounds)
½ cup kosher salt
¼ cup freshly ground black pepper
1 recipe Owensboro Black Dip (page 71)

Sprinkle the salt and pepper on the meat and rub it in. Refrigerate the meat overnight in a plastic bag. Bring the meat to room
temperature and barbecue it meat-side up at 210–240°, mopping it every hour with dip thinned 3-to-1 with water. When
the internal temperature reaches 190–195° (roughly 6–8 hours),
remove the meat from heat and let it rest for at least 30 minutes.
Slice it, chop it roughly, or pull it with a fork or your fingers.

Serve it with dip as a table sauce (use sparingly), with Kain-
tuck Corn Cakes (page 90) and Bluegrass State Burgoo (page 78)
on the side.

Seven Jay Barbecued Goat

Not long ago the Wall Street Journal *observed that the "meat of the moment" was* capretto *(Italian for young goat), because its "richness and deep complexity" had been discovered by celebrity chefs from coast to coast. But goat meat's deep complexity isn't news in Texas, home to all but one of the twenty-one U.S. counties where goats outnumber people. A half dozen or so goat-cooking festivals and competitions are held in the Lone Star State each year (Electra's has been going since 1977), goat is one of the categories at the International Barbecue Cook-Off in Taylor, and the World Championship Goat Cook-Off is held every year in Brady.*

Want to give it a try? First get a goat. Ask around at a farmers' market, carniceria Mexicana, *or halal butcher. These directions are for cooking a young one with the hide and the head removed and a dressed weight of around 20 pounds. You can go up to 60 pounds dressed weight, but if you do, increase the quantities below. The goat can be halved, quartered, or further dismembered, if needed to fit your cooker.*

Tejanos have long been cooking cabrito al pastor *(young goat, shepherd's style) with a spicy, oniony-garlicky mop and serving it with* pico de gallo, *but this is a Protestant version, adapted from what Hawley and Barbara Jernigan of the Seven Jay Ranch near Mullin, Texas, call Papa's barbecued goat. Cowboys cook with direct heat on a grill elevated a couple of feet above the coals, but you can use indirect heat, with smoke from wood chunks (use oak if you have it).*

1 (20-pound) (dressed weight) goat
2 cups melted butter, melted bacon drippings,
or a combination

FOR THE BRINE (OPTIONAL BUT RECOMMENDED)
Approximately 3 gallons water
1 cup cider vinegar
3 cups kosher salt
4 or 5 lemons, halved

FOR THE RUB
2 cups kosher salt
2 tablespoons freshly ground black pepper
2 teaspoons chipotle powder
2 teaspoons ground cumin

FOR THE GLAZE
2 cups sugar, or to taste
1 cup prepared yellow mustard
½ cup cider vinegar
1 teaspoon kosher salt
1 teaspoon freshly ground black pepper

If brining: Combine the water, salt, and vinegar. Squeeze the lemon halves, and add the juice and squeezed halves to the mixture. Seal the meat and brine in a cooler or sturdy plastic bag for at least 1 hour (better is to refrigerate overnight or longer). Remove the meat from the brine and pat it dry.

Combine the rub ingredients, mix thoroughly, and apply generously to the meat. Let the meat sit at room temperature for at least 1 hour before cooking. Cook the goat, meaty side up, at 220–250°, brushing every hour and a half with butter or drippings.

Combine and heat the glaze ingredients, mixing thoroughly (do not boil). Cook the meat to 175° if slicing, 190° if pulling (maybe 9 or 10 hours).

When the meat reaches the desired temperature, brush both sides liberally with glaze, "so it will set," and return it to the heat for 15–20 minutes. Remove from heat and let it rest 20–30 minutes. Serve sliced or pulled.

Barbecued Baloney Sandwiches

Something about the humble bologna sausage brings out the joker in people. Chef Chris Schlesinger argues facetiously that this "latest example of a lowly piece of meat turned into a delicious, if rather unusual, delight" may be "the cutting edge of new barbecue." Another pitmaster-restaurateur, Mike Mills, likes to serve people what he calls "Canadian loin back sausage." When they get a funny look on their faces, he says, "Tastes just like baloney, doesn't it?" Oklahomans proudly call this treat Okie steak or Oklahoma prime rib, but in fact it's found on menus and dinner tables as far east as western Kentucky. In Memphis it's a specialty at well-known joints like the Cozy Corner and the Bar-B-Q Shop.

Elmer's BBQ in Tulsa uses barbecued bologna in a monster sandwich with link sausage and chopped brisket, and elsewhere in the Southwest a baloney sandwich can involve condiments like chopped onions and dill pickles. I think it's best, though, served Memphis-style, as in this recipe. Meat, sauce, and slaw come together on a soft bun to produce what food writer Michael Stern calls "a delicious piggy mess." They laughed when I took baloney out of my cooker—But when they took a bite!—

Most barbecue joints use just grocery-store lunch meat (usually pork adulterated with chicken), but this recipe may be marginally better if you start with good bologna. Pork is traditional, but kosher or some other all-beef bologna is good, too. An entire bologna can run as much as 10-12 pounds, but most delis will sell you a length by weight. If your bologna is a fat one, with a diameter of 6 inches or so, slice it in half lengthwise. (Leave a slimmer one intact—it will be prettier.)

Keep in mind that the meat's already cooked, so you're not really barbecuing it, just flavoring and smoking it. This recipe calls for slicing it before cooking, just to expose more surface to rub and smoke. The meat can go into your cooker as soon as the coals are completely lit. If you're cooking something else as well, it can ride the temperature curve all the way up to normal barbecuing temperature, but if bologna's all you're cooking, why not stop at a lower temperature to let it hang out with the smoke longer? (Doing the same thing with Spam is said to produce good results, but that's wrong in so many ways. . . .)

MAKES ENOUGH FOR 9–15 REGULAR SANDWICHES
OR 6–10 SUPERSIZED ONES

A big chunk (maybe 3–5 pounds) of unsliced bologna
Memphis Pork Rub (page 53)
Vegetable oil
Cheap hamburger buns
Sweet red barbecue sauce—e.g., River City Sauce (page 65)
Creamy or mustard-based coleslaw (pages 83 and 84)

Cut bologna into slices ½–¾ inch thick. Rub or spray the slices with vegetable oil and apply the dry rub lightly. Cook at a low temperature (see above) to an internal temperature of 150–160°, 1½ hours or more.

When ready to eat, fry or grill slices to caramelize them a bit, and serve them hot, on hamburger buns with sauce and slaw. Leftover slices freeze well.

St. Louis Hog Snoots

London's St. John restaurant won a Michelin star in 2009 for its innovative "nose-to-tail" menu, but strange pork dishes are nothing new to Southerners. Although these days snoot (i.e., snout) sandwiches have pretty much retreated to a heartland in and around Saint Louis, in the 1930s this everything-but-the-squeal dish was found in black neighborhoods across the South, including Memphis's Beale Street.

Slathered with barbecue sauce and served on white bread, snoots are very fatty, about the size of a salad plate, and weigh in at about a pound. "Not as challenging as chitterlings," is Dotty Griffith's faint praise. She describes the taste as "an intriguing mix of grease, sweet, hot, acid, and tang—not altogether pleasant." The texture, she says, is something like that of a rawhide dog toy.

If you have a problem with the idea of eating a hog's nostrils and facial skin, you shouldn't think too much about your next hotdog, but I confess that this is the one recipe in this book that I didn't test myself. This is adapted from Griffith's book, Celebrating Barbecue.

1 SNOOT SERVES 1–2 PEOPLE
(MORE IF THEY FIND IT DISGUSTING)

Hog snoots, rinsed and dried
2 or more slices of white bread per snoot
Kaycee "Red Menace" Sauce (page 68), Marshallville, Georgia,
    Literary Sauce (page 63), or any sweet, red grocery-store
    sauce (hell, it doesn't matter: You're putting it on *hog snoots*)

Remove the tendons and excess fat. Score the fat side. Place the snoots meat-side down, directly over a low charcoal fire, with the grill at the maximum distance. Close the lid and cook for 10–15 minutes. Check occasionally, and move the snoots away from the coals if they're burning. Turn them over and continue cooking. (Add lit coals as necessary.) Try not to turn the meat more than 2–3 times.

When most of the fat is rendered and the snoots are crisp (about 2–2½ hours), brush them with barbecue sauce and continue to cook, turning them once, for another 10–15 minutes.

Remove the snoots from the grill. Cut them into strips with kitchen shears and pile the strips on sauce-covered white bread. Serve this mess as a sandwich, but eat one strip at a time with bread.

Memphis Barbecue Pizza
and Spaghetti

Memphis is famous for weird barbecue dishes, and these Italo-Memphian concoctions are a couple of the strangest. You could say that they exemplify multicultural syncretism (if you say that sort of thing) and both are unexpectedly good uses for barbecued pork shoulder.

Barbecue pizza came into being in the 1950s as part of restaurateur Horest Coletta's attempt to introduce the pizza pie to Memphis. To get skeptical locals to try the alien dish, Coletta used barbecue sauce instead of marinara and piled on the barbecued pork shoulder. I won't bother with a recipe, because that's it. The result was Elvis's favorite pizza: Priscilla often came by Coletta's for takeout and occasionally the King and his entourage took a private room. Others have imitated Coletta's innovation (even Pizza Hut had a go), but the original is still the greatest.

Barbecue spaghetti is a similar conceit, dating from about the same time. It was probably first served by former railroad cook Brady Vincent at Brady and Lil's (now the Bar-B-Q Shop), but it has also spread throughout Memphis. Barbecue spaghetti is to spaghetti Bolognese as Cincinnati chili is to the Tex-Mex variety—and, as in Cincinnati chili, the pasta should be yieldingly soft, not al dente.

1 pint River City Sauce (page 65), if you want, but store-
   bought is fine for this
1 cup sugar
1 cup chopped onions
3/4 cup chopped green peppers
1/2 cup vegetable oil
1/4 teaspoon kosher salt
2 pounds spaghettoni (thick spaghetti) or vermicelli
Approximately 2 pounds barbecued pork shoulder,
   coarsely chopped

Combine the ingredients except the pasta and the meat in a saucepan and cook slowly, about 30 minutes, until the onions are translucent and the peppers are tender.

Meanwhile, add the pasta to a generous quantity of generously salted boiling water. Boil it gently for 15 minutes, rinse in cold water, and drain. Pour the sauce over the pasta and stir. Put chunks of barbecued pork shoulder on top of each serving, and serve hot.

Cajun Barbecue

People who say that South Louisiana isn't barbecue country are wrong. Folks there just don't call it that. About the only difference between Louisiana andouille and Texas sausage is more garlic. Just so, cochon de lait is nothing but Cajun whole-hog barbecue: Cajuns even cook it at an event called a "cochon de lait," just the way other Southerners cook barbecue at an event called a barbecue.

Cochon de lait means suckling pig, and the traditional method is to suspend a whole one in a rotating frame a few feet in front of a hardwood fire. You can find instructions on the web for building such an apparatus from an old swing set, but before you commit yourself to all that hardware, why not try a scaled-back version to make sure it's worth it?

If you and your cooker can handle a headless piglet and you can find one, go for it. But this recipe is for the abridged version that a number of New Orleans restaurants are serving these days: just barbecued shoulder or Boston butt, studded with garlic cloves and spiced Cajun style. You don't get the crackling skin (and of course many Cajuns swear that's the best part), but this approach may be more suited to urban life.

*You can use the meat to produce a reasonable facsimile of the po'boy that Walker's Southern Style Bar-B-Que has sold for many years at Jazz Fest. (*Times-Picayune *food writer Bret Anderson says that Walker's po'boy has largely created the demand for "a previously obscure Louisiana dish.") Just pile some meat on the nearest thing you can find to a New Orleans French bread bullet — fluffy inside is the key and a Mexican* bolillo *is close — then dress it with chopped cabbage and a dollop of sauce (see below).*

Store-bought Cajun rub is fine (Tony Chachere's and Zatarain's are particularly good), but if you want to make your own, I've provided a recipe.

Bone-in Boston butt, 6–8 pounds
1 or 2 large garlic cloves, halved, per pound of meat
1/2 cup Cajun rub (commercial or from below)

Cut slits in the meat 1–2 inches deep, 3–4 inches apart. Insert a garlic half and some rub in each. Apply the rub generously to the meat, patting it in. Put the meat in a sealed bag and refrigerate it for 24–48 hours. Cook at 210–250° to 190° internal temperature (should take about an hour per pound). Trim the fat, discard the bone, and shred or roughly chop the meat.

FOR THE RUB (MAKES ABOUT 2/3 CUP)
1/3 cup kosher salt
2 tablespoons freshly ground black pepper
4 teaspoons cayenne pepper
4 teaspoons chili powder
1 teaspoon garlic powder
1 teaspoon onion powder
1/2 teaspoon thyme
1/2 teaspoon sweet basil
1/2 teaspoon bay leaf
1/4 teaspoon MSG

Put the ingredients in a blender and blend to a fine powder.

Generous pinch of garlic powder
Scant 2 teaspoons spicy brown mustard (Zatarain's, if you
   can get it)
1 recipe North Alabama White Sauce, strangely enough
   (page 70)

Add the garlic powder and mustard to the sauce and stir to
combine.

Panhandle Smoked Mullet

Although Swansboro, North Carolina, appears to have the oldest festival honoring the mullet (annual since 1954), this trash fish is particularly identified with the Gulf Coast. Florida these days offers festivals from Niceville to Goodland, and every year the Flora-Bama Lounge on Perdido Key hosts the Interstate Mullet Toss, in which contestants throw dead mullets across the Florida-Alabama line.

One of the best ways to prepare this oily bottom-feeder is to smoke it, and those pre-Columbian Indians in the Caribbean were probably cooking mullet on their barbacoa. Historically, smoked mullet was a common lunch for turpentine hands and other workingmen, and it still has a special place in the hearts of many Southerners from coastal areas, especially African Americans. As Tampa chef Greg Baker observes, it's "kind of our de facto barbecue dish." Cooked low and slow with hickory smoke, it certainly meets the criteria. Mullet is bony, so it doesn't make good sandwiches, but mixed with whipped cream cheese and maybe some sweet hot sauce, the smoked fish makes a dandy spread. Or you can just separate the meat, dip it in a sauce like the one below, and eat it with your fingers.

The taste? Well, let's just say that if you want a fish that tastes like fish, mullet is for you. Recently the supply has been threatened by state restrictions on the fisheries. (The Wakulla County court ruled that since mullets are the only fish with gizzards they're actually birds, not subject to the regulations, but this view did not prevail.) There's also a voracious Asian market for mullet roe, sold as an aphrodisiac. Nevertheless, you can still buy smoked mullet all over the Florida Panhandle. I think it tastes best from places like Mineral Springs Seafood in Panacea, where the smoker sits in the parking lot and perfumes the Coastal Highway. If you can get fresh fish, of course, you can smoke your own. But freshness is important. "Because mullet is an oily-fleshed fish," John T. Edge observes, "two-day-old mullet is not considered trash fish; it's considered trash."

Here's how they smoke mullet at the Boggy Bayou Mullet Festival in Niceville. (The same technique works for any oily fish: In the Southern mountains it's used for trout.)

SERVES 6 (1 MULLET EACH)

FOR THE MULLET
6 medium-size (1–3 pound) mullets
1 pound hickory chips (not chunks)
1 cup kosher salt
1 gallon water
¼ cup olive oil

FOR THE BOGGY BAYOU FESTIVAL DIPPING SAUCE
(MAKES ABOUT 1½ CUPS)
½ cup honey
½ cup yellow mustard
⅓ cup cider vinegar
¼ cup Worcestershire sauce
1 tablespoon hot sauce
2 tablespoons chopped parsley

Soak the wood chips overnight, and drain them.

Remove the heads and innards from the fish, split them from head to tail, and rinse them under running water until clean. Dissolve the salt in the water and brine the fish, refrigerated, for 30–60 minutes. Remove the fish from the brine and dry them. Place them skin-side down on a well-oiled grill and baste them with the olive oil.

Use only a few coals to keep the temperature low. Cover the coals with ⅓ of the chips and add more as needed, to keep the smoke coming. Cook the fish approximately 1 hour at 150–175°, or 30–45 minutes at 200°. The fish are done when the cut surface is golden brown and the flesh flakes easily when tested with a fork.

For the dipping sauce, blend the honey and mustard in a saucepan, then stir in the remaining ingredients. Bring the mixture to a boil, remove it from the heat, and let it cool.

Smoked mullets can be kept in the refrigerator for 2–3 days or in the freezer for up to 3 months.

Rubs

In days of yore, it was common to add flavor to barbecue by mopping it while it cooked, but when cooking with indirect heat, opening the cooking chamber frequently to mop can be a problem, so many barbecue cooks now use flavorful rubs instead. Rubs also help to create a tasty "bark" on pork shoulders and chicken skin. Ingredients almost always include salt and some element of heat: black pepper, cayenne, paprika, or a combination. There's often something from the onion-garlic family, and other spices. Cumin, mustard, and celery seed are popular, or just seasoned salt or chili powder. Sugar is not universal, but common—yet another reason to cook "low and slow" (at temperatures over 250° or so, sugar turns black and ugly). After you've tried some of these, you can devise your own secret formula.

All-Purpose Rub

Many rub recipes, like most of those that follow this one, are for particular kinds of meat, but here's an all-purpose rub that's good with everything from chicken to pork, beef to bologna. Shoot, it's even good on popcorn.

MAKES A BIT LESS THAN 3 CUPS

¾ cup packed light brown sugar

½ cup kosher salt

½ cup sweet paprika

¼ cup seasoned salt (such as Lawry's)

¼ cup freshly ground black pepper

2 tablespoons cayenne pepper

2 tablespoons onion powder

2 tablespoons garlic powder

2 tablespoons chili powder

1 tablespoon ground cumin

Mix the ingredients thoroughly. This keeps indefinitely, sealed and refrigerated.

Texas Beef Rub

You've got to love Texans' respect for the meat. A Texas rub can be just a simple "Dalmatian" rub of salt and black pepper. There's often some paprika or cayenne for a little heat, though, as in this recipe. Many Texans—Kreuz Market in Lockhart, for example— let it go at that, but fooling around with the optional additions below doesn't mean you're an effete weenie. (Adding a lot of sugar might.)

MAKES 1 ½–2 CUPS

½ cup kosher salt

½ cup freshly ground black pepper

¼ cup paprika

1 tablespoon cayenne pepper, or to taste

2 tablespoons dry mustard (optional)

¼ cup onion powder or garlic powder, or half-and-half
(optional)

1 tablespoon chili powder, Mexene brand if you can get it
(optional)

1 tablespoon ground cumin (optional)

Mix the ingredients thoroughly. Keeps indefinitely when refrigerated in a sealed container.

Kansas City Rub

Kansas Citians have a sweet tooth that won't quit. Not only are their sauces (e.g., Kaycee "Red Menace" Sauce, page 68) just about the sweetest going, sugar is the largest component of most of their rubs—more than a third of this one, for example. Notice that if you added a cup of the sweet stuff to Texas Beef Rub (page 51), this is pretty much what you'd get.

This was designed for ribs, but it can be used on just about any-thing.

MAKES A BIT LESS THAN 3 CUPS

---

1 cup sugar

¾ cup paprika

6 tablespoons kosher salt

¼ cup black pepper

3 tablespoons garlic powder

2 tablespoons chili powder

1 teaspoon cayenne pepper

Mix the ingredients thoroughly. Leftover rub can be sealed and kept indefinitely.

Memphis Pork Rub

Memphis is situated at a latitude almost exactly midway between those of Austin and Kansas City, and its barbecue rub splits the difference, too. Here's a typical example—sweeter than Texas; hotter than Kansas City. Use it for Pan-Southern Pork Shoulders (page 16), Righteous Ribs (page 18), or Barbecued Baloney Sandwiches (page 36).

MAKES ABOUT 2 CUPS

1 cup paprika

½ cup packed light brown sugar

¼ cup kosher salt

2 tablespoons freshly ground black pepper

2 tablespoons onion powder

1 tablespoon cayenne pepper

1 tablespoon garlic powder

1 tablespoon dry mustard

1 tablespoon celery salt

2 teaspoons MSG (optional)

Mix the ingredients thoroughly. Keeps indefinitely when refrigerated in a sealed container.

Memphis-Hellenic "Dry Rib" Rub

In 1948 Charlie Vergos, owner of the Rendezvous in Memphis, began serving ribs rubbed with a spicy powder instead of with sauce, and he really started something. Today in Memphis "dry" ribs are at least as popular as ordinary "wet" ones. Vergos's original dry ribs are unusual, cooked with direct heat relatively hot and fast at 350° or so, which makes them chewier and less smoky than ribs barbecued the usual way. The dry ribs at most other places are cooked like ordinary "wet" ones, just powdered with additional rub instead of sauced.

The Rendezvous's secret rub owes something to Vergos's Greek heritage, with lots of seeds and twigs and things. One effort at reverse-engineering includes crushed oregano and thyme and a half dozen kinds of seeds—also chili, onion, and garlic powders, lots of paprika, allspice, sugar, salt, pepper, MSG. . . . In other words, it's a production. (That MSG? You'd be surprised how many commercial sauces and competition barbecuers add it. There's a reason for that.) Fortunately for counterfeiters, the rubs at other Memphis rib joints are less complicated. The one below is simplified but still Hellenic-inflected.

Apply this rub generously to ribs before cooking them, and dust them with it before serving.

½ cup paprika

½ cup packed light brown sugar

6 tablespoons chili powder

6 tablespoons celery salt

¼ cup ground cumin

¼ cup kosher salt

¼ cup freshly ground black pepper

8 teaspoons onion powder

8 teaspoons dry thyme or oregano or a mixture

4 teaspoons dry mustard

4 teaspoons cayenne pepper

Combine all the ingredients, mixing thoroughly. If tightly sealed and refrigerated, this can be kept indefinitely.

Sauces and Mops

Barbecue is barbecue before any sauce goes on it (except maybe in Missouri). But it is universally acknowledged (except maybe in Texas) that seasoning can be added in liquid form. That's what those Caribbean Indians were doing with their lime juice and pepper. Many sauces have the same ingredients as mops that have fallen into disuse; in fact, you can thin them and use them to mop, if you want to.

Founding Fathers' Sauce

Colonial and antebellum Americans liked their barbecue like their skillets—good and greasy—so they mopped it with butter or lard. Before the introduction of cayenne around the dawn of the nineteenth-century, alternating mops of that and salt water was about all they did.

These days butter and fat have largely disappeared from mops and sauces, but (cardiovascular health considerations aside) maybe we've made a mistake. To see what really old-fashioned barbecue might have tasted like, try this cayenne-free sauce with pork, beef, or mutton. It's adapted from Smoke & Spice, *by Cheryl Alters Jamison and Bill Jamison.*

MAKES ABOUT 1 ½ CUPS

---

6 tablespoons melted bacon drippings

6 tablespoons melted butter

1 tablespoon onion powder, or 1 medium onion, chopped very fine

½ cup white vinegar

Juice of 2 lemons

2 tablespoons Worcestershire sauce

2 teaspoons freshly ground black pepper

1 teaspoon dry mustard

1 teaspoon kosher salt

Combine the ingredients and mix thoroughly. Serve this hot as a table sauce (stir before spooning over meat), or add it, heated, to meat while pulling or chopping. It will keep indefinitely in the refrigerator.

The Mother Sauce

This is the ur-sauce, ubiquitous in the nineteenth-century United States, and still found in conservative places like eastern North Carolina that don't cotton to this new-fangled "ketchup" goop. Barbecue guru Steven Raichlen calls it "the original kick-ass sauce, designed to complement pork, not camouflage it." In fact, in the old days it was used with all kinds of meat, not just pork. Wesley Jones, a former slave from South Carolina, remembered using it in the 1850s to "anoint" goats, hogs, sheep, and sides of beef.

Often some melted butter or lard was added to the mix to replace the fat lost in cooking, and of course everyone dropped in a pinch of "secret ingredients." (Mr. Jones added some sage, coriander, basil, onion, and garlic.) We're less likely now to regard lost fat as a bad thing, and the secret ingredients were probably as much for mystique as for flavor, so most people these days use something like the recipe below. There's one mutation you might want to consider, however. "Some folks drop a little sugar in it," Mr. Jones reported, and replacing the black pepper with sugar or molasses produces a sweet-and-sour version that many people prefer to the fierce original.

Use this with pulled pork shoulder and you can pretend you're at the front end of an East Carolina whole-hog pig-picking.

MAKES ABOUT 1 GALLON

---

1 gallon cider vinegar
¾ cup crushed red pepper
¼ cup kosher salt
2 tablespoons cayenne pepper
2 tablespoons freshly ground black pepper (or 1 cup packed
   light brown sugar—see above)

Mix the ingredients and let stand at least 4 hours. Use this as a mop while cooking and then serve it as a table sauce to be sprinkled (sparingly!) over the pulled or chopped meat.

Piedmont Dip

North Carolinians in the Piedmont, between the flatlands of the coastal plain and the high country of the mountains, sauce their pork with a vinegar-and-pepper "dip" that has some ketchup in it, as do their Piedmont cousins in South Carolina. (Kentuckians also call their barbecue sauce "dip," a word that apparently comes from "dipney," itself a word not used since the late nineteenth century.)

The added ketchup, a departure from eastern orthodoxy, has occasioned a lot of hoohah in the Tar Heel State, but the truth is that the two styles are more like each other than either is like what is found in the mountains and beyond. If you replace half the vinegar in eastern North Carolina's Mother Sauce (see the previous recipe) with a 50:50 mixture of ketchup and water, and dial back the heat a bit, the result is this recipe—pretty much what you get at several famous barbecue places in Lexington, North Carolina, and vicinity. It's still thin, and the dominant note is still vinegar.

You can stop right there if you want, and maybe neophytes should. But in the Piedmont additions are common and, within limits, not discouraged. Try adding 2–3 tablespoons of Worcestershire sauce, for instance, or 1–2 tablespoons of dried mustard (not so much that it turns the sauce yellow, like the next recipe). Or express yourself with a touch of the powders (chili, onion, garlic) or paprika, or even a pinch of ground cloves. . . . You get the idea.

2 quarts cider vinegar
1 quart ketchup
1 quart water
¼ cup kosher salt
1 tablespoon crushed red pepper
1 tablespoon cayenne pepper
1 tablespoon freshly ground black pepper
¼ cup packed light brown sugar

Mix the ingredients in a saucepan and bring the mixture to a boil. Reduce the heat and simmer for 10–15 minutes. Sprinkle a bit on meat while pulling or chopping, and serve it as a table sauce. This keeps in the refrigerator indefinitely.

Sandlapper Yellow Sauce

Many folks have been known to add a bit of dry or prepared mustard to a sauce, to give it a bit of a bite, but only in a stretch of South Carolina from Columbia to the coast do they add so much that the sauce turns an alarming school-bus yellow. Maurice Bessinger's Piggy Park in Columbia is the biggest and best-known yellow-sauce establishment; Hite's in Leesville may be the best.

The bare-bones version of this sauce is just the vinegar-and-pepper Mother Sauce (page 59) with mustard added (lots of mustard). Although the original had no sugar, most people these days add some. Aside from that, the most common enhancement is Worcestershire sauce, tomato in some form, or both, as here. This can be served as a table sauce, mixed in as you chop or pull shoulder, or slathered on ribs. But take it easy: this is strong stuff.

MAKES ABOUT 3 CUPS

1½ cups prepared yellow mustard

1 cup cider vinegar

¼ cup ketchup

Up to 4 tablespoons packed light brown sugar, to taste
(optional)

2 tablespoons Worcestershire sauce

2 teaspoons hot sauce

1 teaspoon kosher salt

Combine the ingredients and mix thoroughly. This is best if cured overnight in the refrigerator. It will keep indefinitely if refrigerated.

Marshallville, Georgia, Literary Sauce

Readers of a literary bent may recognize John Donald Wade as one of the "Twelve Southerners" who wrote a book called I'll Take My Stand *in 1930. This sauce went on his favorite barbecue, and it's hard to get more Southern than that. Wade got his barbecue from a black woman named Lottie Jones who ran a barbecue place in his hometown of Marshallville, Georgia. In the days of Jim Crow, Mrs. Jones sold take-out barbecue in paper sacks to white customers, and her sauce was so popular that in 1962 the Marshallville Garden Club put her recipe in their cookbook,* What's Cooking in Marshallville?*

If you ever wondered why diabetes is a problem in the Deep South—well, with more than a cup of white sugar in every pint this is even sweeter than Kansas City sauces. It's so sweet I want to put it on ice cream, but if you want to put it on your pork or chicken, its provenance can't be beat.

MAKES A BIT LESS THAN 2 QUARTS

---

1 (24-ounce) bottle ketchup
3 ounces hot sauce
2 pounds sugar (this is not a misprint!)
1 pint cider vinegar
1 (8-ounce) can tomato sauce
½ teaspoon cayenne pepper, or to taste
½ teaspoon kosher salt
½ teaspoon freshly ground black pepper
2 lemons, halved
2 slices white bread, chopped or blended into crumbs

Combine the first 8 ingredients in a saucepan. Squeeze the lemons and add the juice and halves to the sauce. Stir in the bread crumbs. Bring the mixture to a boil, then reduce the heat and simmer for 10 minutes. This freezes well.

The Lord's Own Alabama Rib Sauce

In 1958 "Big Daddy" Bishop founded Dreamland, a legendary barbecue joint in Tuscaloosa that serves nothing but ribs and white bread. Just about that time, he said, the Lord came to him in a dream and gave him the sauce recipe. Naturally the recipe is secret, so unless the Lord shares it with you, you'll have to make do with this facsimile, from The Ultimate Barbecue Sauce Cookbook, *by Jim Auchmutey and Susan Puckett.*

MAKES A BIT MORE THAN 2 QUARTS

1 (28-ounce) can tomato purée

⅓ cup prepared yellow mustard

3 cups water

1½ cups cider vinegar

¼ cup dark corn syrup

2 tablespoons fresh lemon juice

2 tablespoons sugar

2 tablespoons packed light brown sugar

2 tablespoons chili powder

1 tablespoon dry mustard

1 tablespoon paprika

2 teaspoons cayenne pepper

1 teaspoon kosher salt

1 teaspoon freshly ground black pepper

½ teaspoon garlic powder

Whisk the tomato purée and mustard together in a saucepan until smooth. Stir in the other ingredients. Bring the mixture to a boil, reduce the heat, and simmer for 30 minutes, stirring occasionally. This is best served warm. It will keep, refrigerated, for several weeks.

River City Sauce

Just as Memphis rubs (page 53) sort of split the difference between Texas and Kansas City, so a typical Memphis barbecue sauce is kind of like what's served in Kansas City (page 68), but thinner and less sweet, with some of the heat and vinegar of a piedmont North Carolina dip (page 60). Here's a typical specimen.

MAKES ABOUT 1 QUART

1½ cups ketchup
1 cup cider vinegar
½ cup water
¼ cup molasses
2 tablespoons packed dark brown sugar
2 tablespoons butter
1½ tablespoons prepared yellow mustard
1 tablespoon onion flakes
1 tablespoon Worcestershire sauce
2 teaspoons chili powder
½ teaspoon cayenne pepper
½ teaspoon garlic powder
½ teaspoon kosher salt
½ teaspoon freshly ground black pepper

Combine the ingredients in a saucepan and bring them to a boil over medium heat. Reduce the heat and simmer for 15–20 minutes, stirring often. Cool and serve. This freezes well.

Lone Star Sauce and Mop

The meat markets of central Texas used to let their smoky meat speak for itself. Sure, you might mop it with its own drippings, maybe laced with a bit of cayenne, but you didn't mess with Texas barbecue by saucing it. Under the baleful influence of Kansas City, you can now get thick, sweet, red sauce in Texas, but old-timey places still serve your meat stark naked, and if you want sauce (as you might, if it's poorly cooked and dry) at most you'll get a thin liquor comprising drippings, a little ketchup and vinegar, a touch of cayenne and a few other spices, with not much sugar, if any. Originally devised for brisket, these sauces are now used with steaks, ribs, chops, sausage, pulled pork, cabrito—even turkey and chicken.

This recipe, adapted from one in Gary Wiviott's Low & Slow, *resembles the sauce at Cooper's Old-Time Pit Bar-B-Que in Llano. At Cooper's you point at the meat you want and they slice off some for you. On request, they'll dunk it in a bucket of sauce. If you don't have a bucket for your sauce, you can put a bottle on the table and let folks drizzle it on.*

You can thin this 4:1 with beer, water, or stock and use it as a mop while cooking. That's a good idea if you're cooking with direct heat, but it's not really necessary with indirect heat.

2 cups beef, veal, or chicken stock (meat drippings
     if you have them)
¼ cup bacon fat
2 cups ketchup
2 cups white vinegar
1 tablespoon hot sauce
1 tablespoon Worcestershire sauce
2 teaspoons freshly ground black pepper
1 teaspoon garlic powder
1 teaspoon onion powder
½ teaspoon kosher salt

Combine the ingredients in a saucepan and simmer for 20 minutes over medium heat, stirring occasionally. Serve warm. This keeps indefinitely in the refrigerator.

Kaycee "Red Menace" Sauce

Barbecue sauce is important in Missouri. St. Louis leads the nation in per capita sauce consumption, and Kansas City even hosts an annual sauce contest. Perhaps that's why when most Americans hear "barbecue sauce" they think of the Missouri version—what you find at your grocery store, at chain restaurants, and on a McRib, for that matter. Oddly, you don't find it at the Kansas City place that local boy Calvin Trillin famously declared to be "the single best restaurant in the world," Arthur Bryant's Barbecue, where the idiosyncratic sauce is long on the flavors of vinegar, black pepper, and onion. For a "Kansas City–style" sauce—tomato-based and very sweet, with a touch of heat—check out Bryant's longtime rival, Gates and Sons Bar-B-Q.

Ollie Gates says his sauce tastes good on broccoli. Cynics would say it tastes good on cardboard, and that's why some of us don't quite approve of it: You can't really taste the meat it goes on. As Gary Wiviott says, sauces like Gates's "can cover a multitude of sins," so this is what to use if you've burned the chicken or undercooked the ribs. Food writer Hanna Raskin calls it a "sauce combover." Barbecue blogger Meathead Goldwyn agrees; he says that sauces like these ("ketchup on steroids") don't penetrate the meat and "sit on top like frosting." But he adds that when used as mops in the final minutes of cooking they caramelize well and add a nice glaze to ribs and chicken.

Here's an utterly typical Kansas City sauce, a lot like what Gates and Sons has served since 1946. (The bourbon's not typical, but makes the sauce a lot more interesting.)

1 quart ketchup
1 cup water
¾ cup white vinegar
½ cup packed dark brown sugar
½ cup bourbon whiskey (optional—see above)
2 tablespoons chili powder
2 tablespoons molasses
1 tablespoon freshly ground black pepper
1½ teaspoons onion powder
1½ teaspoons garlic powder
1 teaspoon cayenne pepper, or to taste
1 teaspoon kosher salt

Combine the ingredients in a saucepan and bring them to a boil over moderate heat. Reduce the heat and simmer for 25–30 minutes, stirring often. This freezes well.

North Alabama White Sauce

One of barbecue's microregions is centered on Decatur, Alabama, where legendary barbecue man Big Bob Gibson started dunking his barbecued chickens in a vat of tangy mayonnaise-based sauce in the 1930s. Today this kind of sauce is common in North Alabama, but elsewhere it's found only as an imported oddity. Big Bob's restaurant is still in business and still literally submerging freshly barbecued chickens in this stuff, but you can slather, if it's easier. The sauce can also be used as a marinade or mop, and in Alabama it's now even used with meats other than chicken, but let's not get carried away.

There are lots of versions of Big Bob's sauce out there, but this one is the next thing to authorized, since it comes from Big Bob Gibson's BBQ Book *by Chris Lilly, who married the man's great-granddaughter and runs the restaurant today.*

MAKES JUST SHORT OF 1 QUART

---

2 cups mayonnaise

1 cup white vinegar

½ cup apple juice

2 teaspoons prepared horseradish

2 teaspoons freshly ground black pepper

2 teaspoons fresh lemon juice

1 teaspoon kosher salt

½ teaspoon cayenne pepper

Combine the ingredients in a large bowl and mix well. Use the sauce immediately or refrigerate it. It can be stored in the refrigerator, sealed, for up to 2 weeks.

Owensboro Black Dip

Folks around Owensboro, Kentucky, do not fear bold flavors. They douse their greasy mutton barbecue (page 31) with a pungent "dip" that can stand up to the gamey meat. It gets its color and its name from the Worcestershire sauce that is its principal ingredient. This dip is similar to the table sauce at Owensboro's Moonlight Bar-B-Q Inn. It can also be thinned with 3 parts of water to 1 and used to mop the meat while it's cooking.

If you find a use for it other than to conceal the taste of mutton, please let me know.

MAKES ABOUT 1 QUART

2 cups Worcestershire sauce

1½ cups white vinegar

¼ cup fresh lemon juice

¼ cup packed dark brown sugar

2 tablespoons kosher salt

1 tablespoon freshly ground black pepper

1 teaspoon garlic powder

1 teaspoon onion salt

1 teaspoon allspice

1 teaspoon MSG (optional)

Combine the ingredients in a saucepan and bring to a boil; reduce the heat and simmer for 10–15 minutes. Serve it hot or at room temperature. This can be saved indefinitely in the refrigerator.

Side Stews

One of the many barbecue traditions that survive along the Atlantic coast and in Kentucky is serving some sort of meat stew as a side dish. These dishes vary widely, but they usually have more than just a little taste in common with the barbecue they accompany, bringing yet another dose of meaty goodness to the plate.

Virginia-Carolina "Yes, We Can" Brunswick Stew

Brunswick stew was originally just a hunter's stew, where you would throw whatever was in the day's bag into the stewpot with vegetables from the garden. In fact, the Indians of the Southeast had similar stews, so the endless argument between Virginians and Georgians about who invented Brunswick stew should really be just about who named it (the Virginians have the better argument). Anyway, it's a curious fact that North Carolinians probably eat more Brunswick stew, per capita, than either of them, because Tar Heels just scoff it up as a side dish with barbecue, like coleslaw, rather than treating it as a grand ceremonial production reserved for special occasions.

Like barbecue hash (page 76) and burgoo (page 78), Brunswick stew varies wildly from cook to cook. The feds say that if you want to sell stew in interstate commerce and call it "Brunswick," it has to contain at least two meats. That used to mean squirrel and the like, but these days it's usually chicken, with beef and/or pork. There are no laws about the vegetables, but in Virginia and North Carolina they almost always include corn, butter beans or limas, tomatoes, and onions. After that you're on your own. The finest stew recipe I know can be found in The Bacon Cookbook, *by North Carolinian Jim Villas, but here's a trashier version, entirely from cans yet surprisingly not bad, adapted from a recipe devised by my pal Gary Freeze. If you've got a squirrel or a rabbit, go ahead and throw it in, too. Obviously, no additional salt is required.*

1 (12½-ounce) can (or more) chunk chicken, drained and
   shredded with fingers
1 (13.7-ounce) carton chicken broth
1 (15¼-ounce) can whole-kernel corn, with liquid
1 (15-ounce) can Dinty Moore beef stew, meat shredded
   and potatoes roughly mashed with fingers
1 (15-ounce) can lima beans, drained
1 (14½-ounce) can petit-cut diced tomatoes, drained
1 (14½-ounce) can diced new potatoes, drained
1 teaspoon onion powder
Dash of hot sauce (chipotle is good, but not required)
Several grinds of black pepper

Combine the ingredients in a stockpot and bring to a boil.
Reduce heat and simmer, uncovered, until the tomatoes are
thoroughly cooked and the consistency is no longer soupy.
(This can also be done in a crockpot.) Serve hot. This freezes
well.

South of the Border Barbecue Hash

"Barbecue hash" is the meat side dish for barbecue in South Caro-
lina and parts of Georgia. Originally a way to use hog's heads,
haslets (heart, liver, and lungs), kidneys, and other viscera at hog-
killing time, it has evolved to the point where many people don't
know that it ever included offal at all. In the antebellum version,
you just threw the entrails into a large cast-iron pot along with
some more conventional pork (shoulder or ham) or even beef, and
boiled it, stirring constantly, until it fell apart. Then you removed
any bones, seasoned it, and kept cooking until it became a sort
of meat slurry, which was served over rice. These days, tomatoes,
potatoes, and onions are common additions, and some baroque
versions are hard to distinguish from Brunswick stew.

This version calls for a Dutch oven or a stockpot, so you can
have the full hands-on experience, but it can be easily adapted for
a crockpot. If you want that organ-meat taste and can't get pork
liver, you can substitute calves' liver, or even chicken livers. If you
don't want that taste, use chuck roast.

MAKES A BIT MORE THAN 3 QUARTS

---

3 pounds pork shoulder or butt, cut into 2-inch cubes
1 pound pork liver (or other liver, or chuck roast),
    cut into 2-inch cubes
1 large onion, finely diced (optional)
3 large baking potatoes, peeled and chunked (optional)
1 (28-ounce) can peeled tomatoes, drained and chopped
    (optional)
1½ cups mustard-based barbecue sauce (page 62)
4 tablespoons butter
1–2 teaspoons freshly ground black pepper
Kosher salt, to taste
Cooked white rice

Brown the meat in an oiled pot. Cover the meat with water and bring it to a boil. Reduce the heat and cook at a low boil until the meat falls apart. Add the onions, potatoes, and tomatoes (if desired) and continue to boil until the potatoes are soft.

Run the mixture through a food grinder or mash it with a potato masher. Stir in the barbecue sauce, butter, and pepper, and season with salt; cook it to the consistency of spaghetti sauce. Serve hot, over white rice.

Bluegrass State Burgoo

Kentuckians like to say that burgoo is more a concept than a recipe, but it usually includes two or three meats, some corn and onions, and other vegetables—in other words, burgoo is just Kentucky's version of Brunswick stew, and the only reason to include a separate recipe for it is that mutton has traditionally been one of the meats in the mutton-'cue area around Owensboro. The formula for the Moonlight Bar-B-Q Inn's sauce is on page 71, and here's their burgoo recipe.

You can do a lot to this before it stops being burgoo. Vary the ratio of beef to mutton (or lamb), to suit your taste. Got game? Use it. Throw in some tomatoes, or butter beans, or okra. Crank up the cayenne, or omit it. Leave the ingredients identifiable or cook them down to a mush. (A burgoo cooked in the 1880s was described as "a homogeneous liquid, about the consistency of molasses.") The truth is, there are probably more versions than cooks, since many cooks never cook the same stew twice.

MAKES A BIT MORE THAN 6 QUARTS

1 pound mutton (or lamb) shoulder

1 pound beef stew meat

2 pounds bone-in chicken (buy a cut-up 4-pound chicken,
   cut one up yourself, or double the recipe)

2 cups shredded or finely chopped cabbage

1 cup finely chopped onion

2½ pounds potatoes, peeled and cut into ¼-inch dice

1 (16-ounce) package frozen corn or 1 cup fresh corn

3 tablespoons ketchup

1 cup tomato paste

Juice of ½ lemon

3 tablespoons white vinegar

¼ cup Worcestershire sauce

4 teaspoons kosher salt, or to taste
1 tablespoon freshly ground black pepper
½ teaspoon cayenne pepper

Boil the mutton and beef until tender, 2–3 hours. Remove the bones, if any, and chop the meat fine. Boil the chicken in 1 gallon of water until tender. Remove the chicken from the pot and add the cabbage, onions, potatoes, corn, ketchup, and 2 quarts of water to the chicken broth. Bring the mixture to a boil, then reduce the heat and simmer, covered.

Meanwhile, remove the bones and skin from the chicken and chop the meat fine. When the potatoes are tender, add the chicken and other meats, then the remaining ingredients. Simmer the mixture for 2 hours or longer, stirring occasionally as it thickens.

Slaws

When German and Dutch settlers came down the Great
Wagon Road from Pennsylvania in the 1700s to settle
the Southern interior, they brought along their "cabbage
salad" (*krautsalat* in German, but *koolsla* in Dutch),
and someone noticed very early on that it was the ideal
sidekick for wood-cooked pork: *The Kentucky House-
wife* (1839) contained what may be the first printed
"cold slaugh" recipe and recommended serving it with
barbecued shoat. Now in much of the South some sort
of slaw has become almost a universal accompaniment to barbecue, either on the side or (in a sandwich)
on top.

Cold Slaugh

Early slaw was essentially pickled cabbage, suitable for an age without refrigeration. That's still a good choice if you're going to let it sit around awhile, and many people prefer it to mayonnaise-based slaw anyway. It's on the menus of many barbecue restaurants, especially in the swath of the South from central Kentucky southward, either as the house slaw or as an alternative to the creamy variety. This recipe resembles what's served at the Whitt's Barbecue chain in North Alabama and Middle Tennessee.

SERVES 5–8

---

1 medium head cabbage, chopped (5–6 cups)

6 tablespoons sugar

½ cup vinegar (cider, white, or half-and-half)

½ teaspoon kosher salt

Pinch of black pepper

Combine the sugar and cabbage and stir to "bruise." Add the other ingredients and toss to mix. Refrigerate for at least 3–4 hours (overnight is better), before serving.

Creamy Coleslaw

These days most Americans think "coleslaw" means cabbage with a creamy mayonnaise-based dressing, like what you buy in a tub at the grocery store. This is a slaw like Debbie Reynolds in a 1950s movie—mild, sweet, unexciting, reliable—and sometimes that's exactly what you want in a supporting role. Here's an unassuming slaw guaranteed not to upstage anybody's barbecue. Before the introduction of bottled mayonnaise in the first and second decades of the twentieth century, this kind of slaw would have been prepared only by home cooks prepared to make their own mayo, but something like it has now become the house slaw everywhere from Bob Sykes's BarB-Q in Bessemer, Alabama, to the late Boyd 'N Son Bar-B-Q in Kansas City.

By the way, if you're one of those folks who like onion in their slaw, be warned that the taste gets stronger as the slaw ages.

SERVES 6–9

1 cup mayonnaise

¼ cup milk

2 tablespoons white vinegar

2 tablespoons sugar

2 tablespoons grated onion (optional)

1 teaspoon celery seeds

½ teaspoon kosher salt

½ teaspoon freshly ground black pepper

1 medium head cabbage, shredded (5–6 cups)

1 large carrot, shredded

Mix the dressing ingredients thoroughly. Pour them over the cabbage and carrot and toss to mix. Refrigerate for at least 3–4 hours (overnight is better) before serving.

Golden Coleslaw

The year 1922 was a big one in barbecue history. Bob Melton started selling pulled pork from his pits in Rocky Mount, North Carolina (two years later he built the state's first sit-down barbecue restaurant), and Leonard Heuberger opened what may have been the first sit-down barbecue stand in Memphis, selling 5-cent barbecue sandwiches. Melton and Heuberger were both pioneers whose places became barbecue landmarks. Melton's closed in 2003 after Hurricane Floyd did it in, but Leonard's, relocated and expanded, is still cooking.

By sheer coincidence, the two places served similar coleslaws that seem to have established local precedents: to this day, most slaw dressings in Memphis and eastern North Carolina include yellow mustard. In some, it's the major ingredient—half or more by volume; in others, it's a mere trace that barely colors the dressing. This recipe is something of a cross between Melton's sweet, intensely mustardy slaw and the milder, creamier slaw from Wilber Shirley's restaurant, down the road in Goldsboro, where Wilber insists, "You gotta have coleslaw. I won't even sell somebody a barbecue unless they get coleslaw. If they want a barbecue and they don't want coleslaw, there's something wrong with that person. It all goes together."

½ cup mayonnaise (or whipped salad dressing)
5 tablespoons prepared yellow mustard
¼ cup sugar
3 tablespoons white vinegar
¼ teaspoon celery seed
Pinch of dry mustard
Pinch of kosher salt
1 medium head cabbage, shredded (5–6 cups)

Mix the dressing ingredients thoroughly. Pour them over the cabbage and toss to mix. Refrigerate for at least 3–4 hours (overnight is better) before serving.

Lexington Barbecue Slaw

In the 1920s Miss Dell Yarborough was working in the Lexington, North Carolina, restaurant owned by her brother-in-law, Sid Weaver, when she introduced the barbecue-eating world to an unusual vinegar slaw, based on what her family ate at home. Most of the barbecue-eating world wasn't interested, but Miss Dell's "barbecue slaw" caught on in the North Carolina Piedmont, where it remains the side dish of choice to this day. (Stamey's in Greensboro still serves the original recipe.)

In some ways this is a throw-back, basically just an old-fashioned vinegar-marinated "cold slaugh" (page 82) with some tomato added—and some heat. In most of the South, coleslaw serves as a cooling contrast to the heat of barbecue sauce, but Piedmont slaw is, in effect, made with barbecue sauce. This is a typical example, based on the one served at Lexington Barbecue. Compare the ingredients in its dressing to those in Piedmont "dip" (page 60), and you'll see that they're just about the same; only the proportions differ.

SERVES 5–8

¼ cup ketchup

3 tablespoons sugar

1 tablespoon cider vinegar

½ teaspoon kosher salt

½ teaspoon freshly ground black pepper

1 generous dash hot sauce

1 medium head cabbage, chopped (5–6 cups)

Mix the dressing ingredients thoroughly. Pour them over the cabbage and toss to mix. Refrigerate for at least 3–4 hours (overnight is better) before serving.

Breads

White bread has its place in the barbecue world. Sandwiches usually call for hamburger buns straight from
the cellophane (but see the corn cake recipe on page
90), and some well-known barbecue places offer buns
or sliced loaf bread with a barbecue plate. Rib joints in
particular seem to like sliced bread since it can double
as a napkin. But there's a reason that visiting Union
troops called the South the "Cornfederacy": Especially
with pork—pork barbecue included—the usual bread
has been made from corn. Here are three varieties,
from the most ancient to one that was paired with
barbecue in living memory.

Cornpone

In eastern North Carolina, some old-fashioned places like the Skylight Inn and Bum's in Ayden serve their barbecue with a thin, crispy rectangle of cornpone, the way folks down east have always done. They used to make their pone with fat from the hogs they cooked, but today's hogs are too lean, so they use lard. You should, too. If you don't, you might as well not bother.

This is about what you get in Ayden.

SERVES 8–10

---

4 cups finely ground white cornmeal

2 teaspoons kosher salt

¼ cup lard

4 cups water, or more if needed

Preheat the oven to 500°. Melt the lard in a 9 × 13-inch baking pan in the preheating oven. Combine the cornmeal and salt in a bowl, and stir in enough water to make a batter thick enough that you have to spread it a bit, like cake batter. When the oven reaches 500°, remove the pan and add most of the melted lard to the batter, leaving some in the pan. Stir the batter well and pour it into the heated pan. Lower the heat to 450° and bake for about an hour.

Hushpuppies

It's not clear whether Warner Stamey, a barbecue entrepreneur in Greensboro, North Carolina, was the first to serve hushpuppies with barbecue or just popularized the combination, but until he did whatever he did, sometime in the 1950s or so, these little deep-fried doughballs had rarely been found apart from fried fish. But Stamey's innovation certainly caught on in the Tar Heel State. Although some old-timers still prefer white-bread rolls (Stamey's grandson's restaurant still offers them as an alternative) and real old-timers prefer cornpone, most North Carolinians now regard hushpuppies as an integral part of their barbecue tradition.

O.T.'s Barbecue in Apex is long gone, but its memory lingers on, as does its hushpuppy recipe in this adaption. If you prefer a savory version, leave out the sugar (or reduce it by half) and add 1 medium onion, chopped fine.

MAKES 2–3 DOZEN

---

2 cups self-rising cornmeal
1 cup self-rising flour
1 teaspoon kosher salt
2 tablespoons sugar
1 large egg, beaten
¾ cup milk, plus more as needed
Lard for frying (peanut oil, if you insist)

Sift the dry ingredients together. Stir in the egg and milk, adding more milk if needed for a firm but workable batter. Heat the lard to 375°. Using a tablespoon, drop walnut-to-golf-ball-sized blobs of batter into the lard. Fry only a few at a time to golden brown, turning if necessary. Drain them on a paper towel.

Kaintuck Corn Cakes

Up a notch in sophistication from pone in the spectrum of Southern cornbreads are these fried batter cakes, which add egg, milk, and baking powder to the basic hoecake. They are, in fact, just cornmeal pancakes, and any left over are good with butter and sorghum for breakfast. They're ubiquitous in the South, but in Middle Tennessee and (especially) Kentucky they're often served with barbecue, either on the side or as the top and bottom of a barbecue sandwich (with sauce and slaw).

If you want to replicate the corn cakes served at most barbecue places, use whole milk and regular grocery-store cornmeal, but buttermilk and stone-ground meal do make for a superior product. (If you don't have buttermilk, add 1 tablespoon each of lemon juice and cider vinegar to 2½ cups of whole milk, let the mixture curdle, and you'll have enough for this recipe.) You can use melted butter instead of bacon grease, but your flavor will suffer. Some northern Kentuckians use yellow cornmeal instead of white, but they're practically Yankees, and probably put sugar in their cornbread, too.

MAKES 24–28 CAKES

2 cups white stone-ground cornmeal

2 tablespoons all-purpose flour

2 teaspoons baking powder

1 teaspoon baking soda

1 teaspoon kosher salt

2 eggs, beaten

2 tablespoons bacon drippings, melted

Approximately 2 cups buttermilk (as needed)

¼ cup cooking oil or lard

Mix the dry ingredients thoroughly. Stir in the eggs and drippings, then enough buttermilk to produce the consistency of pancake batter. Heat the oil or lard in a skillet or griddle over medium heat and spoon on 2-tablespoon batches of batter. When bubbles on top begin to burst, lift the cake to check: When the underside is brown, turn it and cook the other side.

Other Side Dishes

Many other dishes can go with barbecue, but don't
have to. Lots of barbecue restaurants these days offer
french fries. Places on the meat-and-three side of
things might have greens, or macaroni and cheese.
Nothing extraordinary about any of those. But here
are five recipes that are completely ordinary in some
locales but would be odd, if not weird, in others.

Barbecue Baked Beans

Baked beans weren't really a Southern thing until the canned variety came along in the twentieth century, but now the Bush Brothers company in Dandridge, Tennessee, is the nation's leading producer. They're still not usually a barbecue side dish in the conservative Atlantic states, but they've found a place on menus from the mountains to the Mississippi and beyond, to Kansas City. Barbecue places and home cooks alike usually start with canned beans and add stuff like onion, mustard, ketchup, and brown sugar or molasses, but aside from that, there are really no rules.

Bob Sammons, a serious competition barbecuer who works a day job as a psychiatrist in Colorado, has shared a typical recipe from his North Carolina grandmother. He adds the optional ingredients at the end to jazz it up.

SERVES 5–7

---

2 cans (about 32 ounces) pork and beans
3 bacon strips, fried, drippings reserved
1 medium onion, chopped
1 garlic clove, minced
1 tablespoon Worcestershire sauce
¼ cup packed light brown sugar
½ cup catsup
1 dash hot sauce
½ teaspoon kosher salt
½ teaspoon freshly ground black pepper
Pinch of dried basil

OPTIONAL
2 tablespoons cumin seed
2–3 tablespoons cold coffee
Pinch of oregano

Preheat the oven to 350°. Brown the onions and garlic in the bacon drippings. Put the beans in a mixing bowl, then add the cooked onions and garlic with their grease. Add the remaining ingredients, mix well, and pour the mix into a greased casserole. Crumble the bacon on top, and bake for 45 minutes.

Cowboy Beans

The politics of Massachusetts and Texas anchor some sort of red state/blue state spectrum, and so do their beans. It's hard to imagine beans less like the Boston baked variety than the savory dish known on the Border as frijoles charros. *In Texas and throughout the Southwest they're a frequent accompaniment to barbecued brisket (page 19), and they're also great topped with sliced barbecued sausage (page 25).*

The basic list of ingredients makes for a dish that's just a sort of superior bean-and-bacon soup, so you'll want to dress it up a bit with some of the optional additions. I like mine with the chili powder, tomatoes, and chipotle, but you add what you want. That's the Cowboy Way.

SERVES 5–8

1 pound dried pinto beans
½ pound thick-sliced smoked bacon, diced fine
½ medium onion, chopped
2 garlic cloves, minced
1 tablespoon kosher salt

OPTIONAL ADDITIONS
For heat: 1 jalapeño or canned chipotle pepper (more, to taste), minced
For complexity: 2 tablespoons chili powder (Mexene brand, if you can get it), or 4½ teaspoons chili powder and 1½ teaspoons ground cumin
For color and added umami: 1 (14½-ounce) can diced tomatoes, undrained
For sweetness: 2 teaspoons sugar (or 1 [12-ounce] bottle cola drink)

To take this back to its Mexican roots: 4 teaspoons minced
fresh cilantro sprinkled on top before serving
To make it *"borracho* [drunken] beans": 1 (12-ounce) bottle
of beer

Place the beans in a large stockpot and add water to cover them
by 2 inches. Soak them for 6–8 hours. (Alternatively, bring them
to a boil, boil them for 2 minutes, remove from heat, cover, and
let stand for an hour.) Drain the water, rinse the beans, and refill
the pot to cover the beans by 2 inches.

Put the bacon in a frying pan over low heat and render some
of the fat. Add the onions and garlic, sprinkle with the salt, and
cook with the bacon until they're transparent (5 minutes or so).
Add the bacon, bacon fat, onions, and garlic to the stockpot.
Bring to a boil, reduce the heat, add any of the optional ingredients, and simmer for 2–3 hours until the beans are tender. The
mix should be somewhat soupy.

Mississippi-Arkansas Hot Tamales

You might well ask why Greenville, Mississippi, calls itself the Hot Tamale Capital of the World. The answer is that tamales, strangely, have been a popular treat in parts of Mississippi, Louisiana, and Arkansas since the early twentieth century. The most common explanation is that they were brought in by Mexican migrant workers hired to work in the cotton fields, but if so, there's been some evolution. These are not your Mexican tamales. They're skinnier, they're usually made with yellow cornmeal instead of masa, and they're as likely to be wrapped in parchment paper as in the traditional corn husks.

However they got there, by mid-twentieth century tamales were being sold on the street, by vendors at railroad stations, and in little hole-in-the-wall shops in the Delta and vicinity. They also began to appear as appetizers and side dishes on the menus of restaurants, and they're in this book because sometimes they show up in barbecue places: Germantown Commissary in Memphis, for example, or McClard's Bar-B-Q in Hot Springs, Arkansas, Bill Clinton's boyhood local. McClard's started in 1928, barbecuing goat, and although it doesn't serve goat anymore, it does serve tamales. You can get them as a regular side order like slaw or french fries, but real men go for a train wreck called the Tamale Spread, a combination of tamales, beans, barbecued beef, onions, cheese, sauce, and Fritos.

This recipe is close to McClard's, and it's good. The cayenne pepper may not be needed if your chili powder is hot enough. Taste before you add it.

MAKES 20–24 TAMALES

FOR THE FILLING
1½ pounds ground chuck
2 tablespoons bacon fat
1 cup beef broth

½ cup chili powder

1½ teaspoons kosher salt

1½ teaspoons cumin

1 teaspoon garlic powder

1–2 pinches of cayenne pepper, or to taste (optional)

FOR THE DOUGH

3 cups yellow cornmeal

¾ cup lard

2 teaspoons kosher salt

1½ teaspoons baking powder

Up to 3 cups beef broth

20–24 (8 × 5-inch) rectangles of parchment paper
  (or corn husks, soaked in hot water until soft, if you're
  a traditionalist)

Brown the beef in the bacon fat. Add the other filling ingredients and simmer uncovered until thickened (about 20 minutes), stirring often to avoid burning. Set the mixture aside. (This can be made in advance.)

Stir the cornmeal, lard, salt, and baking powder until well mixed. Gradually add the beef broth, mixing with your hands until the dough has the consistency of mashed potatoes, moist enough to spread evenly.

Spread the dough in the middle of a wrapper, lengthwise, and trim it with a knife blade to leave ¾–1 inch on all sides for folding. Spoon 2–3 tablespoons of filling down the middle, and roll the wrapper into an 8-inch-long cylinder. Fold the ends over to seal. Repeat until the dough or the filling runs out.

Stand the assembled tamales on end in a steamer and steam until the dough is firm (60–90 minutes). Serve warm. (Unwrap them before eating.)

New Braunfels Potato Salad

The German heritage of central Texas is reflected not just in its brisket and sausage barbecue but in its potato salad. Mustard, pickles, and vinegar or pickle brine are almost universal. Bacon's not uncommon, either, although maybe not when the potato salad is served as a side dish with barbecue, as it often is in Texas. Sweet or dill pickle has long been a matter of taste, if not debate: this recipe offers a choice, but you can mix them up—or, for a racy nouvelle-fusion alternative, replace some of them with pickled jalapeños.

MAKES ABOUT 12 NORMAL- OR
8 TEXAS-SIZE SERVINGS

---

3 pounds russet potatoes, peeled and cut into ¾-inch chunks

¼ cup dill or sweet pickle juice

1 teaspoon kosher salt, divided, plus more to taste

4 eggs

½ medium sweet onion, chopped

2 stalks celery, diced

3 tablespoons finely chopped dill or sweet pickles

¼ cup mayonnaise

3 tablespoons prepared yellow mustard

1 teaspoon freshly ground black pepper

½ teaspoon paprika (optional)

Cover the potatoes with salted cold water and bring them to a boil. Simmer until tender but still firm (10–20 minutes). Drain and rinse in cold water. Toss with the pickle juice and salt. Chill them in a refrigerator for at least a half hour.

Cover the eggs with cold water and bring them to a boil. Remove from heat, cover, and let stand for 10–12 minutes. Drain, cool, peel, and chop them.

In a mixing bowl, combine the potatoes, eggs, onions, celery, and pickles. In a separate bowl mix the mayonnaise, mustard, pepper, and the remaining salt; add this to the salad and stir gently to mix, adding additional salt to taste. Sprinkle with paprika, if desired. Refrigerate until served.

East Carolina Boiled Potatoes

Boiled potatoes are seldom served with barbecue except in eastern North Carolina, but there they are, more often than not. Your basic, boring, boiled spud can be a pleasing contrast to the heat-and-sour of the region's barbecue sauce (page 59), but some easterners serve potatoes that are, like the Piedmont's slaw (page 86), vehicles for delivering even more vinegar, salt, and red pepper. Potatoes that are a bit mushy absorb more of the pungent cooking liquid, so this recipe calls for boiling what are usually baking potatoes. For authenticity, the hot sauce should be Texas Pete, but any grocery-store brand will do.

SERVES 6–9

---

3 pounds russet potatoes, peeled and cut into
  1½–2-inch chunks
½ cup ketchup
½ cup cider vinegar
2 tablespoons hot sauce
2 tablespoons bacon drippings
1 tablespoon sugar
2 teaspoons kosher salt
1 teaspoon freshly ground black pepper

Put all of the ingredients in a pot with just enough water to cover the potatoes. Bring to a boil, cover, and simmer until the potatoes are beginning to fall apart (45 minutes or more). Remove from heat and let stand for at least half an hour, until ready to serve. Reheat if necessary.

Desserts

As far as I know, there's nothing mandatory anywhere about desserts after barbecue. In fact, many eaters probably prefer just to eat more barbecue. But if you want some sweet relief, here are three dishes that traditionally end a barbecue meal.

Dori's Peach Cobbler

Peaches have been grown from Virginia to Texas, for a long time (Jefferson had them at Monticello), and cobbler has long been a popular use for them. In fact, what may be the first published reference to a cobbler by that name is a recipe for "a Peach pot pie, or cobler, as it is often termed" in an 1839 Kentucky cookbook. Today peach cobbler and barbecue go together all the way from Troutman's in Denton, North Carolina, to Louie Mueller's in Taylor, Texas.

Dori Sanders is a South Carolina peach farmer and novelist, and Dori Sanders' Country Cooking *includes one of the best cobbler recipes going. That it's also the easiest is a bonus. This is what's called a "magic" cobbler, because it creates its own top crust. As my wife once remarked, pork shoulder's not the only thing with delicious "outside brown." Frozen peaches work fine in this recipe, but eschew the canned ones.*

SERVES 6–8

½ cup unsalted butter, melted

1 cup all-purpose flour

2 cups sugar, divided

1 tablespoon baking powder

Pinch of kosher salt

1 cup milk

4 cups frozen peaches, thawed, or fresh ones, peeled and
    thinly sliced (5–6 medium peaches)

1 tablespoon fresh lemon juice

Several dashes ground cinnamon or ground nutmeg (optional)

Preheat the oven to 375°. Pour the melted butter into a 13 × 9 × 2-inch baking dish. Combine the flour, 1 cup of the sugar, the baking powder, and the salt. Mix well and stir in the milk, mixing just until combined. Pour this batter over the butter, but do not stir them together.

Combine the peaches, lemon juice, and the remaining sugar and bring the mixture to a boil over high heat, stirring constantly. Pour the mixture over the batter, but do not stir together. Sprinkle with the cinnamon or nutmeg, if desired.

Bake for 40–50 minutes or until the top is golden brown. This is best served warm, with vanilla ice cream, but it's good cold, too.

Nilla Wafer Banana Pudding

Banana pudding, another classic finale to a barbecue meal, has been around roughly as long as vanilla wafers. Soon after Nabisco began selling those cookies in 1901 someone used them in a banana trifle, and by 1920 or so the recipe was on the box. It's still there, virtually unchanged. Somehow or other, banana pudding got associated with the South; when you find it somewhere else, it's usually in a Southern-themed restaurant.

These days many home cooks and barbecue places use instant vanilla pudding and even frozen whipped topping. Wilber's in Goldsboro, North Carolina, is one of them. Wilber Shirley told Greg Johnson and Vince Staten, the authors of Real Barbecue, *"People think it's a complicated recipe, and I don't tell them otherwise. There ain't nothing to it. My granddaughter could make it if she didn't eat all the cookies first."*

But you don't need a recipe for that, so here's the original Nabisco recipe, cooked a little slower is all. Personally, I prefer whipped cream to the meringue topping called for here—but you don't need a recipe for whipped cream, either.

SERVES 8

¾ cup sugar, divided
3 tablespoons all-purpose flour
Dash of kosher salt
1 whole egg
3 eggs, separated
2 cups milk
½ teaspoon vanilla extract
45 vanilla wafers, plus more for garnish, if desired
5 ripe bananas, sliced, plus more for garnish, if desired

Combine ½ cup of the sugar with the flour and salt in the top of a double boiler. Mix in the whole egg, the egg yolks, and the milk. Cook the mixture, uncovered, over boiling water, stirring constantly, until thickened, 10–12 minutes. Remove it from heat and stir in the vanilla extract.

Spread a small amount in the bottom of a 1½-quart casserole. Top with a single layer wafers, then a single layer of banana slices, then about ⅓ of the custard. Repeat: wafers, bananas, custard. Repeat again.

Beat the egg whites at the mixer's high speed until soft peaks form. Gradually add the remaining sugar and beat until stiff peaks form. Spread over the custard to the edge of the dish. Bake at 350° until lightly browned (15–20 minutes).

Serve warm or chilled. Top with additional wafers and banana slices before serving, if desired.

Pig-Pickin' Cake

Although North Carolinians have been going to pig-pickings since colonial days, the widespread use of the expression "pig-picking" dates only from around 1970. Soon after that, though, this variation on Pineapple Dream Cake began to appear in Tar Heel church and community cookbooks as "Pig-Pickin' Cake."

The list of ingredients lowers the tone of even this book, but it provides some sweet relief to the vinegary tang of Tar Heel barbecue. Here's the version pitmaster Corbette Capps got from some Baptists.

SERVES ABOUT 24

FOR THE CAKE

1 box yellow cake mix (Corbette likes Duncan Hines)

4 eggs

¾ cup vegetable oil

1 (5½–6 ounce) can mandarin oranges

FOR THE TOPPING

1 (9-ounce) carton frozen whipped topping

1 (3.4-ounce) box instant vanilla pudding mix

1 (5½–6 ounce) can crushed pineapple

½ cup chopped pecans and/or ¼ cup flaked coconut
   (optional)

Preheat the oven to 325°. Grease and flour three 8- or 9-inch cake pans or a 13 × 9 × 2-inch baking pan. Add the eggs and oil to the cake mix and beat for about 2 minutes. Add the orange slices with juice and beat for about 1 minute. Pour the mixture into the pans and bake for 20–30 minutes. Cool thoroughly.

Combine the topping ingredients and whip until fluffy. Spread the topping between the cake layers and on top of the cake. Sprinkle pecans and/or coconut on top, if desired. Keep the cake refrigerated.

To Drink

Beer can be really good with barbecue, especially barbecue with no sauce or a sweet one. Soft drinks are all right, too, or corn liquor. But you don't need recipes for those.

Sweet Tea

The little black dress of barbecue potations is sweet ice tea. It can go with anything, and in barbecue places run by Baptists—often the best—it usually does. It's especially good as a counterpoint to vinegar-based sauces, producing a fine old sweet-and-sour yin-yang.

Here's Fred Thompson's recipe for the house wine of the South, from his book Iced Tea. *If you're feeding diabetics or Yankees, you can leave out the sugar and serve the tea with a syrup of equal parts sugar and water on the side, to be added to taste.*

MAKES 2 QUARTS

---

6 regular-size tea bags
⅛ teaspoon baking soda (a good pinch)
8 cups water, divided
1½–2 cups sugar (if you're a sweet-tea newbie,
    start with 1½ cups)

Place the tea bags and baking soda in a large glass measuring cup or ceramic teapot. Bring 2 cups of the water to a boil and pour over the tea bags. Let steep for 15 minutes.

Remove the tea bags (do not squeeze them: it will add bitterness). Pour the tea into a 2-quart pitcher, add the sugar, and stir until it's almost dissolved. Stir in the remaining water. Let the tea cool, then chill it and serve over ice.

Acknowledgments

My wife and frequent coauthor Dale thought she had ducked this one. When UNC Press asked if we'd be interested in doing this book, I immediately said yes and she immediately said no. I remember her very words: "You're on your own, sport." But Dale good-naturedly sampled every recipe in this book except hog snoots, as well as a great many others that didn't make the cut. Not only that, she read the manuscript and saved me from a number of errors and infelicities. Thanks to her, as always.

A great many other people helped with this little book one way or another. My historical account owes much to Robert Moss, author of *Barbecue: The History of an American Institution*; Robb Walsh, author of *Legends of Texas Barbecue* and other useful books; and Meathead Goldwyn of amazingribs.com. Permission to use recipes or other indispensable help came from Jim Auchmutey and Susan Puckett, Johnny Bell, Corbette Capps, Gary Freeze, Dennis Gilson, Dottie Griffith, Lake High, Cheryl Alters Jamison and Bill Jamison, Hawley and Barbara Jernigan, Chris Lilly, Anne Wade Rittenberry (John Donald Wade's daughter), Bob Sammons, Dori Sanders, Jim Shahin, Fred Thompson, Daniel Vaughn, James Villas, and Gary Wiviott. Thanks to one and all.

Index